P9-ECN-455

BEFORE
THEIR
TIME

Lessons in Living
from Those Born Too Soon

DANIEL TAYLOR
RONALD HOEKSTRA, M.D.

InterVarsity Press
Downers Grove, Illinois

InterVarsity Press
P.O. Box 1400, Downers Grove, IL 60515
World Wide Web: www.ivpress.com
E-mail: mail@ivpress.com

InterVarsity Press® is the book-publishing division of InterVarsity Christian Fellowship/USA®, a student movement active on campus at hundreds of universities, colleges and schools of nursing in the United States of America, and a member movement of the International Fellowship of Evangelical Students. For information about local and regional activities, write Public Relations Dept., InterVarsity Christian Fellowship/USA, 6400 Schroeder Rd., P.O. Box 7895, Madison, WI 53707-7895.

All Scripture quotations, unless otherwise indicated, are taken from the Holy Bible, New International Version®. NIV®. *Copyright ©1973, 1978, 1984 by International Bible Society. Used by permission of Zondervan Publishing House. All rights reserved.*

The photos in this book were taken by friends and family members of the children whose stories are being told. The publishers acknowledge and thank them for their contributions.

Photograph of Daniel Taylor provided by Julia Taylor.
Cover photograph: Christina Rahr

ISBN 0-8308-2265-8

Printed in the United States of America ∞

Library of Congress Cataloging-in-Publication Data

Taylor, Daniel, 1948-
  Before their time: lessons in living from those born too soon/Daniel Taylor, Ronald Hoekstra.
    p. cm.
  Includes bibliographical references.
  ISBN 0-8308-2265-8 (cloth: alk. paper)
  1. Infants (Premature) 2. Birth weight, Low—Complications. 3. Parents—Attitudes. 4. Christian life—Anecdotes.   I. Hoekstra, Ronald, 1942- II. Title.
  RJ250.T39 2000
  618.92'011—dc21
                                                                                    00-039582

18	17	16	15	14	13	12	11	10	9	8	7	6	5	4	3	2	1
14	13	12	11	10	09	08	07	06	05	04	03	02	01	00			

*In gratefulness for the lives of all those born too soon—
those who make it and those who don't—
and for all who love and care for them.*

CONTENTS

Acknowledgments

We would like to acknowledge some of the many people who contributed to this book. First and foremost are the children themselves and their parents who were willing to tell the stories. And we thank the nurses and friends who stood beside them and shared their part with us.

We would like to thank Rodney Clapp and Jeff Crosby for their immediate enthusiasm for the project and Cindy Bunch-Hotaling for her efforts in improving the manuscript. Chelsea DeArmond has earned our gratitude for her long hours of transcribing interview tapes. Thanks also to Carol Rottman for sharing with us her insightful dissertation.

INTRODUCTION

To every thing there is a season,
And a time for every purpose under heaven:
A time to be born, and a time to die.

ECCLESIASTES 3:1-2 KJV

There is a time for everything. Birds point south in the fall, branches and taxes bud in the spring, extended families head home for Thanksgiving, and laughter and tears are welcomed at weddings.

Too soon or too late is trouble. Things that miss their appointed hour are at risk, and they place us at risk. They are out of season, unexpected and therefore unprepared for. They catch us as we are, not as we wish to be. They show us what we do not want to see.

Consider those born too soon—before their time. Forty weeks is the proper time for forming a baby. Thirty-eight or forty-one will do just fine. But not thirty, not twenty-seven and, there can be no doubt, not twenty-two.

This book tells the stories of six children born too soon. Four who were born after only twenty-two weeks of pregnancy, a little more than half the time allotted to form a child in the womb, and a set of twins born at twenty-five weeks. This is not enough time to complete the infinitely complex task of weaving a child together. Such a short time causes problems—life-threatening problems. It also creates opportunities—opportunities for courage, friendship, faith and love.

These stories changed every person in them; they may change

you as well. For these are not simply tales of someone else's kids, of interest to those around them but not to the rest of us. These stories raise many of the fundamental questions of life, including some for which our society is desperately searching for answers: What makes a life worth living? When should we begin to treat a life as precious, and how much should we do to preserve it? How much should a society spend to rescue the most fragile? How disabled is too disabled to be encouraged to live? What is the balance between medicine and faith? What roles do prayer and miracles have in the modern, technological world?

These questions are not answered with detailed arguments or statistics or surveys. They are answered, to the extent that they are answered at all, by the stories themselves. Not everyone will take away the same answers or find the same lessons. That's how it is with stories. But our hope is that everyone who reads this book will never again try to answer the questions without thinking of Lamarre, and Simon, and B. J., and Blake, and Anna and Liam.

✳   ✳   ✳

Some of these questions are ancient, but others are new, or are now asked with new urgency. Technology and ethical pluralism give us more choices than we are comfortable with. Those who came before their time a century ago simply died. It was sad, but it required no choosing. Today we can keep alive those some say we shouldn't. And we can refuse to save those we should.

Is there such a thing as a person who shouldn't be alive? Especially someone at the beginning of life? Some think there is. The arguments against saving the extremely premature are serious. It is very expensive to preserve the life of a twenty-two- to twenty-four-week-old infant. A typical three-month stay in the hospital might cost $400,000. Some think the money should be spent elsewhere.

Others emphasize the cost to the child. When the roll call of problems grows longer and longer, and the benefit of treatment seems less and less, difficult questions arise. How much is too much? When are we doing things *to* the baby instead of *for* the baby? When are we simply postponing the inevitable?

The last question presupposes that one knows what will inevitably happen. Anyone who has worked with preemies knows that isn't the case. Some cases look hopeless and turn out well; some look hopeful and turn out tragically. Yet even those who survive have a much higher probability of a broad spectrum of problems that could be with them all their lives: brain damage, chronic lung disease, vision problems, impaired motor and cognitive skills, all of which can lead to significant developmental delays.

We often argue for and against positions today based on our perception of how much someone else will supposedly suffer, even when no actual pain is involved. We even justify the death of the person as being for his or her own good to relieve or avoid suffering. So it is not surprising that we agonize over who and how to treat when life seemingly begins too early.

*   *   *

We know the challenges these children face. There are five major areas of concern for severely premature, low birth-weight babies: cardiovascular, intestine and nutrition, lungs, eyes, and brain.

In extremely premature infants there is a blood vessel, which during the fetal period connects the two major arteries carrying blood away from the heart, that often does not close spontaneously, as it does in full-term infants. The failure of this vessel to close spontaneously can result in low blood pressure and decreased efficiency of the heart, as well as prolonged dependence on a respirator and chronic lung problems. In most cases the infant can be given medicine that will cause the vessel to close, but some require surgery.

Like many other organs, the intestines of these babies are underdeveloped and have the potential for disastrous failures. Perhaps the most dreaded intestinal problem is a perforation resulting in the contents of the intestines spilling into the baby's abdominal cavity. Some perforations are spontaneous, while others may be caused by an inflammation of the bowel—a condition known as necrotizing enterocolitis. At its most severe, this condition may result in a literal rotting away of an infant's intestine.

The lungs of severely premature babies are not ready for normal breathing. Before twenty-three weeks gestation there are very few tiny air sacs in the lungs. The air sacs that are present often are not lined with the slippery material (surfactant) that allows them to remain expanded. These air sacs are the place where oxygen and carbon dioxide are exchanged between the lungs and the baby's blood. Even for several weeks beyond twenty-three weeks gestation, an infant's lungs are so immature that he or she must be given surfactant and kept on a respirator to have a chance to survive.

Ironically, the oxygen supplied to the lungs through a respirator may place the infant's eyes at risk. These babies are born with only partially developed retinas. The extra oxygen required by a premature baby may encourage the abnormal development of blood vessels in the eye. In its most severe form, this can cause the retina to detach and results in blindness.

Finally, and perhaps most frighteningly, is the possibility of hemorrhaging in the brain. A minor hemorrhage may not cause significant problems, but a major one may lead to serious long-term motor and cognitive problems. Doctors grade these hemorrhages on a scale of one to four. A grade one or grade two hemorrhage is considered minor and in most instances does not prevent a good outcome. On the other hand, grade three and grade four hemorrhages are known to greatly increase the risk for long-term developmental problems. This evaluation is done with an ultrasound examination of the brain and is one of many number games the parents and child play—and one of the most important.

So many things can go wrong. Yet the body wants so badly to live that it fights each enemy with all its might. And we must decide what our role in that fight is to be.

Each of these stories rises out of the practice of Dr. Ron Hoekstra at Children's Hospital in Minneapolis, Minnesota, which is associated with Abbot-Northwestern Hospital. All of these babies were born at Abbot-Northwestern and then transferred through a tunnel to Children's Hospital. Dr. Hoekstra is one of a group of twelve neonatologists at Children's Hospital that specializes in the illnesses of newborns, especially in the problems associated with prematurity.

A tall, slim, graying man in his mid-fifties, Dr. Hoekstra speaks quietly and laughs easily. He is self-effacing, preferring the background to the spotlight. To his friends, he is a wonderful combination of intelligence, integrity, compassion and commitment. In the workplace, he makes some people uneasy. They know he is a perfectionist with high expectations for himself and for others who work with these children.

Those expectations came to Dr. Hoekstra early. He was born and reared in Minnesota among people of northern European stock who tend to equate self-worth with hard work. A job done correctly is assumed more than praised, and the devil has a keen appetite for slackers.

Dr. Hoekstra was brought up with equally clear religious expectations in a conservative part of Christendom. As one catechism says, the purpose of human existence is to enjoy God and serve him forever. Dr. Hoekstra was taught to believe both, but Minnesotans generally have an easier time understanding the requirement to serve than to enjoy.

Dr. Hoekstra is now a Presbyterian, but denominations are not important to him. His faith in God is. Though trained to work with the physical, he understands the spiritual as central. Seeing this life as an interweaving of the two, he regards his calling as a doctor as a call to minister to both. That dual calling was clear to him as a young man when he spent time as a doctor in Ethiopia, and it is clear now in the regular trips he makes to Ukraine to do what he can for the great physical and spiritual needs of people there.

In his practice Dr. Hoekstra neither trumpets nor hides his faith. Those he works with generally know where he stands. Some share his commitments, many do not, but most respect the way he lives out his values.

At some point Dr. Hoekstra will indicate to the parents of his patients that he believes God has more to do with the healing of their threatened child than any skill he may have. Some parents show no interest in this observation, while others drink it in like water in the desert. For the former, he tries to be the best medical doctor he can be. For the others, he encourages their belief that there is more at work in their children's lives than biology and the flip of a coin.

Given his willingness to be identified as a person of faith, it is not surprising that some parents feel it is providential that Dr. Hoekstra is assigned to care for their child. One of the mothers in these stories recalled discovering that Dr. Hoekstra was a fellow believer and said, "Obviously that was a great comfort to us."

It is worth asking why this mother, or anyone else, would feel this way. Is it important that someone who performs a service for you shares your core beliefs? Does it hold true for plumbers, car mechanics or real estate agents? Would you rather have a surgeon operate on you who shared your core convictions or one who was first in her medical school class? Is care any less competent or less effective from those doctors and nurses in the unit who are not religious? Is God less able to make use of those who don't particularly believe in or follow him?

Parents of threatened babies are generally not greatly interested in theoretical questions of this kind. A twenty-ounce, twenty-two week infant is at such risk, facing such steep odds, and so delicately balanced on the high wire of life, that any passing breeze of possibility, any nuance of advantage or support or encouragement is welcomed like a desert plant welcomes the dew.

In such a situation, it is no small thing that the doctor treating your child at this moment shares your belief that God cares about your child even more than you do, that healing can come through an imperfectly understood blend of medical skill and spiritual power, that prayer, somehow, someway, works—even if not always to the end we pray toward.

Dr. Hoekstra's faith does not preclude worry. One mother says, "Some doctors are optimists, and some are pessimists. Dr. Hoekstra is an optimist." That assessment would come as a surprise to his family and friends.

Actually, Dr. Hoekstra is a worrier—but a sort of providential worrier. That is, he is a worrier who believes the universe ultimately has a benevolent bent. He knows everything that can go wrong, and he has seen everything go wrong many times. But he has also seen the unexpected good, the unanticipated recovery, the unlooked for healing—the moment of grace. Therefore, he tends not to give up before the patient has.

*   *   *

Much of Dr. Hoekstra's life is spent in the NICU, the neonatal intensive care unit. The NICU is its own world, intersecting the larger world here and there, but existing apart in a slightly altered time and space. One of the first things you notice is its quietness. The nurses mostly wear tennis shoes, moving around so quietly that you can't imagine the shoes ever wearing out. There is often conversation going on, between nurses and doctors, staff and parents, parents with each other, but in low voices and almost always about the business at hand.

And then there are the machines. Each infant lives in a mechanical solar system. Each is a small sun at the epicenter in a clear plastic ark, tiny chest rising and falling, and even tinier fists clenched. A clear plastic tube connected to a respirator is often taped in place in the mouth.

The clear plastic arks are called isolettes. They are yet a smaller world within the world of the NICU. In each lies a knot of tissue and

spirit and potentiality that we call a human life. Our own humanity
is defined in part by the ends to which we will go—or won't go—to
encourage that tiny spark.

From out of the isolettes run lines to the attending machines.
They surround the child like guards around a monarch. They typically include a cardiac-respiratory monitor keeping track of heart
and respiratory rates, and armed with alarms should either become
suspect; a pulse oximeter to monitor the amount of oxygen in the
infant's blood; a respirator to assist in breathing; intravenous infu-
sion pumps to administer fluids and medications; phototherapy
lights to treat jaundice; and a radiant warmer used to keep larger
babies warm.

Some parents love the machines, others hate them, but they all
know that the machines are necessary to keep their child alive.
They yearn for the day their baby will be free of them, but when
that day comes they often fret. They wonder whether the child, so
long sustained by the machines, can now function well without
them.

Into each of these solar systems pass those who care for and care
about the newborn. Each of the most critically ill infants has a
nurse assigned only to him or her. That nurse, almost always a
woman, sometimes chooses which child she wants to work with,
and, therefore, which parents. She becomes what is called the
infant's primary nurse, and any child will have three or more primaries to cover the twenty-four hours of the day.

Nurses are sometimes more closely attached to the child and to
the parents than are the doctors. They spend their entire working
day with one to three babies, and they often know the habits of
each better than those of their own children. Each nurse is highly
experienced in the precarious journeys these babies make in their
bid for life, and each has her own opinions about what should and
should not be done.

Parents of long-hospitalized babies develop their own expertise.
They become skilled at reading the signs. They see in ways they

had never seen before. They learn to see the things the nurses and doctors see—the slightest change of color, the minutest variation in the breathing pattern, the alteration of the reflex, the subtle distension of the tummy. They are more than observers of their child's fate. They play their part in the campaign for life.

Babies, doctors, nurses, parents, machines and God—the NICU is a quietly crowded place. Between the very sophisticated and expensive machines, and the very talented and compassionate people—and with an unquantifiable assist from transcendence—a lot of lives are saved that might otherwise have slipped into eternity with little notice.

But not all lives are saved, and one can never be sure who will make it and who will not. Therefore, the NICU is often a place of quiet drama and heartache and joy—for the newborns, for those who love them and for those who take care of them.

If there are many dramatic moments in the NICU, there are also long stretches of waiting. For many, the long haul poses a greater challenge than the moments of life and death intensity. With the severely premature, there is often no single, one-time crisis. It is not a matter of marshalling forces for "the big operation" or "the next twenty-four hours." When they say the next twenty-four or forty-eight hours are crucial, they mean "Your child may die soon"; they definitely do not mean "If your child gets through this time, then everything will be fine."

In fact, the initial crisis of birth is in some ways the easiest part. Everyone rises to the occasion—parents, grandparents, friends, pastors, prayer chains and medical people. Feelings are intense, attention and prayers are focused. Everyone wants to help. And, God willing, all the help is efficacious and the child lives.

But after the initial crisis passes, and perhaps one or two more in the first couple of weeks, you still have a child that needs three or four more *months* in the womb and isn't going to get them. And therefore, if it lives, it is going to have *many* more months, perhaps years, perhaps a lifetime, of challenges to overcome. And the band will have long since packed up and left.

The one thing all these parents share, especially in the early weeks, is exhaustion. Unfortunately, the extremely premature are a slow-motion crisis in many acts. As one mother said, "It took a long time, but I finally got over the idea that things would be okay once we got through this present problem. No, the crises were not going to be 'over.' It was just going to be one after the other. This was what our life was going to be."

It is in that long, numbing time when values and relationships and character and faith are tested. It is when you have lost track of how many times you've been to the hospital. It is when the adrenaline of the first couple of weeks has worn off, and the long-term weariness of not enough sleep and too much worry has settled into your bones. You try to reenter something like your previous life, but it is now only an *addition* to this new life, not a true return. And you will never see anything quite the same again.

This long step-by-step climb up the mountain would be easier to accept if you knew you were going to get to the top. Mountain climbing may be all uphill, but at least with each step you are higher than the step before. With these babies, the next step might well be off a cliff.

❈   ❈   ❈

These stories by no means convey the totality of what goes on in an NICU. They make no claim to being a statistically balanced cross section of the many thousands of stories that can and should be told. There are no stories here, for instance, of teenage, single mothers with little support, an all-too-common situation in the NICU.

These stories may also be unrepresentative in the degree to which religious faith is at the heart of each of them. These couples were not chosen *because* of their faith, but in each case faith became central to their experience. Perhaps this is because the

NICU is something like a foxhole during an artillery bombardment. If there is any faith in God floating around in a person at all, it will rise to the surface under these conditions.

Finally, there is no claim that these stories are rigorously objective. Each of the people who speaks here has a point of view—an interpretation of his or her experience. It is not necessarily how others involved in the same case would interpret the same events. Some of the judgments may not even be fair, but they are honest.

And of course the authors have a point of view as well. For the most part we have tried to allow these people to tell their own stories, as much as possible in their own words. Our views and values, however, shape what we hear and see, and how we choose to pass it on. Our own commitments are not hard to detect, including our prejudice for the value of every life, and they are made explicit in the final two chapters.

It may be helpful to explain who is telling you these stories. Dr. Hoekstra identified five couples of premature babies who represent a range of experiences. Daniel Taylor interviewed each couple and others who have been involved in or touched by these tiny lives. Since Dr. Hoekstra was one of their doctors, he is inevitably a character within the stories at times, though this is not a book about him.

There is also a narrative voice within each chapter that belongs to Daniel Taylor. That voice describes, reports and reflects. It is hoped that the questions, probings and reflections of that voice either raise issues the reader would like raised or offer insights the reader finds worthwhile.

These stories are just that—stories. They are not clinical case studies or grist for abstract ideologies. They are the true stories of women, men and tiny children exploring the meaning of life, death and faith.

CHAPTER ONE

LAMARRE'S LIST

"We are not human beings having a spiritual experience.
We are spiritual beings having a human experience."

PIERRE TEILHARD DE CHARDIN

J ewel and Anthony Foster had been married one year. The pregnancy had gone wonderfully until the beginning of week twenty-two. At that point the pain began, and it didn't stop.

"Round ligament pain," the doctor said. "Nothing to worry about. Here are some pills." But the pills did no good, and the pain got worse. In fact, it became agonizing—for days on end.

"If it keeps up, I'll put you in the hospital," her doctor said. *If it keeps up, she'll be dead,* Jewel's mother thought to herself.

Finally, they could stand it no longer. Jewel and Anthony went to the doctor's office. He was busy, but they were put into a room. Jewel was bleeding now. The nurse said the doctor had a lot of patients, but he'd be with them soon.

Jewel and Anthony chose this obstetrics practice because they had been told it was one of the best in the Twin Cities. They are a handsome African American couple in their mid-thirties. Anthony is tall, good-looking, soft-spoken and articulate. Jewel has beautiful skin, curly hair and, while equally articulate, is not soft-spoken at all. She is not loud, but Jewel does tell you her mind.

What was on both their minds at this point was Jewel's pain and the fate of their first child.

The doctor finally came in and was quite chipper about the whole thing. "I think you better go to the hospital," he said. "Let me give you the directions."

Anthony was stunned. "The directions? Don't you think she ought to have an ambulance?"

"Oh, ambulances are very expensive. You'll get there just as fast driving yourself."

Anthony thought otherwise. They got an ambulance and labor started on the way.

A perinatologist examined Jewel at the hospital. "We can't stop it now. You're going to deliver." But not anytime soon, he thought, and so he disappeared.

Thirty minutes later the water broke. Fifteen minutes after that Lamarre was on his way into the world. No delivering doctors were present. There was a team of people from the neonatal unit to take Lamarre to intensive care, but they informed Jewel and Anthony, "We don't do deliveries."

Lamarre, however, was coming whether anyone there did deliveries or not. Some obstetrical nurses present delivered the baby.

"Once they saw the head, it got very quiet in the room," Jewel remembers. "It was very hot. He didn't make a sound."

He didn't have what it takes for making sounds. Lamarre was born at twenty-two weeks and weighed twenty ounces. At eleven and one-half inches he was shorter than a ruler—too soon and too small for many neonatology units to even consider trying to save him.

"Don't worry about his not making any noise," one of the nurses said. "His lungs aren't developed. We're breathing for him."

Jewel and Anthony hadn't known enough to realize this was a bad time to be born. They had been told they were past the miscarriage stage, the only problem stage they knew about. They hadn't even been to their first Lamaze class yet. There were still weeks, they had thought, to get the nursery ready, not to mention their minds and hearts.

"We just thought, *Well, he's early,*" Anthony says. "*We'll just put him in the isolette.* We didn't think we'd have any issues."

Lamarre had issues. The first was whether he would live through the weekend. Born on a Friday, there was real doubt that he would ever see a Monday.

The first time Jewel and Anthony saw him after delivery, Lamarre was on a ventilator attached to a plastic tube running to a machine. The endotracheal tube, a piece of plastic about a tenth of an inch across, was inserted into his trachea and was taped to the skin around his mouth. To Anthony, "He didn't look like a baby. He was so small and red. He didn't look like an infant. He looked like an animal baby you would see being born on a nature show on television. He didn't look real."

One of Anthony's first emotions was angry frustration. "My first feeling was, *This is a tragedy. This should not have happened.* We had done all the right things, and now my son was going to have to fight for his life. I was totally upset." They had chosen the best obstetrical practice, and the best had not been good enough. Good planning had not kept Lamarre from coming before his time.

The first life-threatening episode came on Saturday evening, the first full day of Lamarre's life. Anthony and Jewel were sitting in her hospital room, trying to sort through things, when a nurse entered.

"They want you to come to intensive care. There's an emergency."

The trip to intensive care requires going through a long tunnel. Jewel was in a wheelchair, and the nurse was pushing her as fast as she could. They knew they were heading for a crisis, maybe a disaster, and they felt terrible.

What they found when they got to the neonatal intensive care unit was a furious symphony of care conducted by a doctor they had not seen before.

Five nurses and two or three doctors hovered over the enclosed, clear plastic incubator, called an isolette. Bright lights illuminated it in the otherwise darkened room, like an all-night construction zone. Lamarre had been brown and red when he was born. Now he was totally white. His lungs were hemorrhaging. Buzzers were going off on the machines whose lines fed into the isolette. The nurses were handing things around. Dr. Hoekstra had his hands inside the isolette through portholes on the side. He was examining Lamarre's body and looking above his head at the monitors of the machines to which Lamarre was attached. And he was clearly frustrated.

"Where's it at? I need it now. I need it here."

Jewel and Anthony were spectators at this attempt to rescue the life of their son. They were there to be witnesses, not participants. But it is not their style. They are people who act, not watch.

At this point, for Jewel, acting was praying. For Anthony, it was talking to Lamarre.

"The Spirit came over me and said, 'You need to get down there and talk to your son. You can't just stand here and watch him die.' So I got down next to the isolette and I opened this little hole in the corner near his head and I started speaking to him, and I said, 'Lamarre, you're not going anywhere. You've made it this far and you're going to make it. Just keep hanging on.' I was just speaking positive things into that isolette. I was speaking to my son."

Meanwhile, Dr. Hoekstra again said, "I need it now. Why isn't it here?" Whatever he was asking for finally arrived, and he administered it to Lamarre. He kept working the dials on the respirator, calling out orders to the nurses who responded instantly and precisely.

It was a dance with death, or a dance against death. Everything seemed choreographed, but no one knew the final pass. These were the steps we must take, but would Lamarre's body take the corresponding steps? This was our action; what would be his reaction? This was the melody we were trying to play; would he be able to play along?

For ten or fifteen minutes the doctor worked the machines like a pipe organ—adjusting a knob here, altering the flow of medication there. He was focused intensity, directing all his mind and energy to the saving of one life, for at least one more hour, one more night, perhaps for a lifetime.

Finally Dr. Hoekstra stood up straight, removed his hands from the openings in the side of the isolette. "All right, he's stabilized." The color began to flow back into Lamarre, like a spring rain into parched ground.

Jewel was given a new room near the intensive care unit. She and Anthony went to sleep. At 2 a.m., it all happened again. The entire scene was repeated. This would be the nature of their lives.

                              *   *   *

All neonatologists are committed to saving the lives of premature infants. If not, they wouldn't be in the business, which is always much more than a business. But different doctors, with equal skill and commitment to the good of the child, have different ways of trying to accomplish that end.

Some, like Dr. Hoekstra, give equal weight to the spiritual and medical dimensions of healing. Others are pragmatists and scientists. They trust their training, their skills, their experience and their tests. They are the enemy of false hope and wishful thinking. Do everything that is reasonable, but listen when reason says there is nothing helpful left to be done.

It's not hard to predict whom Jewel and Anthony Foster would prefer. They are people who not only believe in miracles but get up most mornings expecting one or two before breakfast. They live in a world in which what we see is only a small part of what actually is. For them, reality is primarily spiritual, not material. It is a battleground for souls, a contest between transcendent forces in which we are both participants and prize.

On that Saturday night, Dr. Hoekstra told them he would not be on duty for the next few days. His partner, Dr. Vicksburg, would be following Lamarre's progress and doing a number of tests. The Fosters, it turns out, are not big fans of tests, especially when tests are seen as determiners of reality.

They first saw Dr. Vicksburg on Sunday morning, after Jewel had been discharged from the hospital. When they came into the NICU, Dr. Vicksburg had just finished examining Lamarre and was washing her hands. After brief introductions she said, "I have the x-rays, and it doesn't look very good at all. We have to talk."

Doctor-parent conferences are an ongoing fact of life in the rhythm of the NICU. This first one for the Fosters was going to set the tone for many to come. When they got into the conference room, Dr. Vicksburg began to list the problems. Lamarre's heart was only pumping at a small fraction of its normal capability, and there was a murmur as well; his lungs were extremely immature, and he would likely develop chronic lung disease were he to live; and, worst of all, he had experienced a grade three to grade four brain hemorrhage, making it extremely likely he would develop severe, long-term neurological problems. All from having been born too soon.

This host of problems led Dr. Vicksburg to open up a topic every doctor wishes was never necessary. "I think you should consider making a decision about what you want to do."

To do?

She told them it was quite likely that Lamarre would not survive. Perhaps the humane thing for their son would be to turn off the respirator and allow him to die in his mother's arms. Jewel recalls the doctor saying, "You can have more children, Jewel."

But Jewel wasn't interested in "more children." She was interested in this child, in Lamarre. And she saw Lamarre and his situation not through the eyes of science and medical tests but through the eyes of faith. "I told her about my belief and my faith in God, and that I was not going to make a decision about Lamarre's life, and if the decision was going to be made, the Lord was going to make it. The decision to disconnect that respirator was not a decision for us to make."

Anthony wasn't so sure.

"I was contemplating it. I was seriously considering it. We were going to have friction. Jewel was going to say, 'I'm going for it,' and I was going to say, 'I don't think we should.' "

Friction was the least of the things Anthony was going to get if he tried to convince Jewel they should give up on Lamarre.

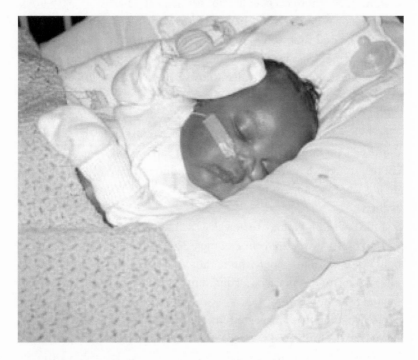

Lamarre Foster in the NICU

Friends played a role as well, according to Anthony.

"I told a buddy about it, and he said, 'There's no way you should do that. There's no way you should pull the plug.' I was telling him what the doctors were saying. He gave me that reassurance. Doctors don't know everything. He built me up when I was almost defeated."

"Pulling the plug" is an unsettling and perhaps unfair phrase. It is not used by most physicians but is an increasing part of our public conversation. It reminds us that our lives sometimes depend on machines, especially at the beginnings and ends of life, and we don't like that dependence. It is a phrase that not only means failure but also implies callousness or calculating indifference.

Nothing could be further from the truth in a neonatal intensive care unit. Nowhere do people fight for lives any harder or with more compassion than in these places. These are men and women who have dedicated themselves to saving those often thought least likely and, by some, least worthy to be saved.

But doctors and nurses also know from sad experience that not every life can be saved. Sometimes it is not courage or caring or even faith that decides who lives and dies. Sometimes it is biology. The body can continue to function despite many imperfections. But there can be one too many or one too large. And when that time comes, it is not a matter of callously "pulling the plug," but of recognizing what is happening and doing what seems best in light of that reality.

But don't talk biology to Jewel. Jewel talks to the great Biologist.

Don't talk "when that time comes" to Anthony, because Anthony believes in a Timekeeper who stands outside of time. These people are not easily discouraged. They have a different notion of what it means to be *realistic*.

So when it was suggested to Jewel that further treatment of Lamarre was futile and perhaps not in his best interest, she told Dr. Vicksburg, "As long as Lamarre will receive what you have to give him, you give it to him. As long as he keeps receiving it, you keep giving it. And then if he doesn't receive it, we'll know. We'll know what to do."

Dr. Vicksburg took a different tack. "You are a strong woman, Jewel. I have children of my own, and I can see how you feel about this. We will give Lamarre what you want. But what if his heart stops? Do you want us to give him CPR?"

"If he receives it, you give it to him."

Doctors and parents both want what is best for the newborn. But sometimes they pull in different directions. Sometimes it feels like war.

Jewel was the commanding general for one side. And Dr. Vicksburg, despite her great concern and compassion for the tiny life in her charge, was perceived as being on the other. "I saw us as advocates for Lamarre and her as an advocate for medical science. She wanted to show us x-rays, but I didn't want to see all that. I wanted to speak for life, not for death."

For Anthony and Jewel it was not a matter of whether Dr. Vicksburg was an excellent doctor with the best of motives; it was a collision of universes, of values, of ways of understanding what is real and what is not.

Jewel, characteristically, saw it as spiritual warfare: "She was operating in the natural realm of medical expertise, and we were looking at it with spiritual eyes. All her training and experience was telling her there was no hope. She seemed sure of what the end result would be. If the heart didn't get him, it was going to be the lungs. She knew. It was simply a fact."

But all facts, all data, require interpretation. A fact is not significant until it is put to use, until it finds its place in a way of thinking, until it has a consequence. The Fosters put the data of x-rays and lab tests and examinations into a different world than did Dr. Vicksburg. The doctor's scientific pragmatism was a red flag to Jewel.

To be fair to Dr. Vicksburg, Dr. Hoekstra does not see her as the Fosters do. He says, "She's an excellent doctor. If I had to choose one doctor to take care of my grandchildren, it would be her."

But to the Fosters, this had nothing to do with medical excellence. They told Dr. Vicksburg that they considered Lamarre's condition a spiritual matter.

"We are going to remain steadfast, and we are not going to waver in our faith in God."

She knew where they stood, and that was the end of the meeting.

"We said, 'We're going to expect a miracle.' And Dr. Vicksburg responded, 'Well, you're going to have to expect a great many of them.' "

*   *   *

Dr. Vicksburg had allies in this tug-of-war. In the days following Dr. Vicksburg's rotation in the NICU, Dr. Anderson took his turn in looking after Lamarre and doing rounds on him. He agreed with Dr. Vicksburg's grim prognosis.

"It doesn't look good. What do you want us to do?"

The Fosters thought they had answered this question.

Dr. Anderson was straightforward. "I've never seen a child with this many problems make it out of the unit."

Jewel asked just how many problems Lamarre had. Dr. Anderson ticked them off. Jewel sensed an opportunity.

"Do you think you could make a list of those problems?"

Dr. Anderson also sensed an opportunity.

"I can do that."

For Dr. Anderson it was an opportunity for the Fosters to actually see in writing the number and severity of Lamarre's problems and perhaps to become more realistic about further treatment.

For Jewel, it was an opportunity to keep track of miracles.

Lamarre's list was impressive. He had most every problem common to the extremely premature infant. No major organ system was unaffected—lung problems, infectious problems, metabolic problems, liver problems, weight problems and, most serious of all, neurologic and bowel problems. Beside the cool, clinical, jargon-filled printed analysis, Dr. Anderson hand wrote additional comments. "Likely to develop chronic lung disease." "Severe hemorrhage—chance of long-term handicap now much higher with hydrocephalus." "Will need intravenous feeding—many babies develop serious life-threatening liver damage from prolonged intravenous feedings."

If this was supposed to make Jewel come to her senses, it only made her return to her core values. Across the top of her copy of Lamarre's list she wrote, "In all things give thanks!" She immediately noticed that of the thirteen items, there was one positive item. By number three, "cardiovascular," Dr. Anderson had written "heart doing well." It was like giving a bloodhound a sniff of the escaped convict's socks.

"It said 'heart doing well.' Lamarre had a strong heart. That was good. A *strong* heart. The Bible says all things begin with the heart, and Dr. Anderson had written that Lamarre has a strong one. I decided that we would start with that, with Lamarre's strong heart, and then we would take care of the rest of the problems one by one."

And as those problems were taken care of, one by one, over the following days, weeks and months, Jewel used Lamarre's list to keep score. Large black X's were scratched over category after category, usually with a date and a few numeric notations. The cross outs seemed not just visual indicators but great sword slashes directed at the spirits of death and disbelief. For the most dangerous items on the list, an X was not enough. In the margins beside those, in Jewel's handwriting, was the word "healed."

But what does "healed" mean? For the Fosters it clearly means more than a biological process that restores health. For them, *healed* means the same thing it meant when Jesus healed the blind man or Namaan was healed of his leprosy. *Healed* means the intervention into daily life and diseased tissues by the personal force that created the cosmos—namely, God.

Not everyone is comfortable with that way of thinking. Even people with religious commitments often prefer to let the natural be natural. When certain things go wrong with your body, there's only so much you can do, and then you die. You might well pray to God for comfort and courage, but bone cancer is bone cancer, and if it gets to a certain stage, then your time is up.

To such people, and certainly to the secularist, talk of miracles is a cue to politely change the subject. It smells of medieval holy rel-

ics, television preachers and backwoods revivals. At best it's irrelevant, and at worst it gets in the way of good medicine.

What does it mean, for instance, to say that Lamarre had been
"healed" of his hydrocephalus? With this condition, cavities in the
brain, called ventricles, fill with fluid. If enough fluid collects, pressure is put on the tissue, causing brain damage. The fluid can be
drained and symptoms may dissipate, but if damage has been done,
then has he been healed or have events simply run their natural
course? And what if there is a small amount of damage, but much
less than one would expect for the level of hemorrhaging? Does that
mean that God protected Lamarre but not quite completely, for
God's own reasons? Or does it mean that there is a range of natural
outcomes for any set of conditions and some babies are simply
luckier than others?

For Jewel, the notion of luck does not apply. "This has nothing to
do with luck. This is a beautiful and very incredible experience we
are going through. The neonatologists were there, assigned by God.
The perinatologist was there, assigned by God. Everyone was there,
assigned by God."

This is not a position that can be successfully argued against,
and most doctors don't try. Some don't argue because they believe
it themselves, others because they believe it can be helpful to the
parents, and still others because they believe the only thing they
really need to focus on is the medical condition of the infant.
Some doctors move alongside the faith of the parents, and others
hold it at a distance. But all work for what they believe is best for
the child.

Simply put, medicine, as a practical science, is not comfortable
with miracles. There is no "Miracles 101" course in medical school.
The whole enterprise of medicine is based on identifying and
responding to natural phenomena. Divine intervention is a wild
card that threatens sober, scientific, reasonable treatment for reasonable conditions.

Some babies, however, push the envelope. Their problems are so great and so many and their chances of beating all of them so remote that *miracle* doesn't seem too sensational a word. Dr. Hoekstra defines a miracle as "surprised by God." "There are kids who should not survive, cannot survive, will not survive—and yet do survive. You stand at their bedside, and you know they are not going to make it. And then you detect a little light in their condition, and then a little more light."

Dr. Hoekstra does not go around the unit calling down miracles or even mentioning them. He knows most of his colleagues would use different language. When they see an unexpected turnaround or unexplainable recovery, they are likely to say, "Well, that was certainly surprising."

Dr. Hoekstra tries to encourage some of these surprises. Neonatologists wash more often than a flea-ridden dog scratches. As they make rounds from isolette to isolette, they wash their hands each time they are going to touch the infant—dozens of time in a day. "I try to make it a rule. Each time I wash up, I pray for the baby in the isolette that I am going to examine. If my partners knew this, they'd have me locked up. But I think praying and asking for wisdom is part of a miracle—to know what to do."

Lamarre, for one, was a kid in need of miracles—or at least a string of surprises. Along with his poor lungs and hemorrhaged brain, Lamarre lost most of his bowel. At the age of eleven days, Lamarre was found to have necrotizing enterocolitis. His bowel was perforated and rotting away.

The doctors had no choice but to remove the decayed portion of the bowel, saving as much as possible. That possible turned out to be minimal. They removed all the ileum portion of the bowel and most of his jejunum. The amount of the small intestine remaining was barely compatible with life. It simply wasn't long enough to absorb adequate nutrition from passing food. Even Dr. Hoekstra wouldn't argue for his chances.

The surgeons attached what was left of the upper part of his bowel directly to his abdominal wall, creating a hole in his side out of which stool could pass. And they waited, fully and reasonably expecting him to die.

But he wouldn't. Some kids are just born uncooperative.

Weeks passed, and then months. Then one of those surprises.

Lamarre started to pass stool out his rectum. It shouldn't have been possible. His intestine was not even hooked up to his rectum. Stool could only come out of his side. It was obvious.

It was obviously wrong. The doctors did a scan using barium to show where things were going. They discovered that the tiny bit of remaining small intestine had spontaneously created an attachment to the large intestine from which it had been cut off. Doctors call such a spontaneous attachment a fistula, and they decided to go along with Lamarre's body on this one.

At four and one-half months they operated a second time on his bowel. Going into the operation, they didn't know how much small intestine Lamarre had left. There had been no measurement in the first operation when the dying bowel was removed, perhaps because he wasn't expected to live anyway.

The average full-term newborn has around 200 centimeters of bowel. An absolute minimum necessary for Lamar to have a chance would be 20 centimeters of small intestine and a functioning ileocecal valve leading to the large intestine. When the surgeons went in, they found, to their surprise, that he had 20 centimeters of small intestine and a functioning ileocecal valve. They closed off the link to the abdominal wall, tied off the fistula and attached the remaining small intestine to the ileocecal valve.

A miracle? Fistulas do happen from time to time. Dr. Hoekstra smiles. "Greatly fortuitous—at the very least."

For the Fosters, Lamarre's overcoming his "list" of problems, including his bowel, was clearly a miracle—and Dr. Hoekstra had no problem with that assessment. For other doctors and parents, it was simply unexpected, maybe even unexplainable, but nothing that was going to alter their view of how the world works.

Jewel and Anthony see it as simply a matter of naming what you

are seeing before your eyes. Anthony says, "The time comes when
you have to speak. When it walks like a duck and quacks like a
duck, then acknowledge it—it's a duck."

But miracles are perceived to have happened only where miracles are accepted, even expected. If miracles are judged impossible
in advance, then no event will be seen as miraculous. Lamarre
shouldn't have made it, but he did. His physical changes could be
measured and documented. What caused them sometimes could
not be. Talk of miracles and divine healings will always give comfort
to some and heartburn to others.

                              *   *   *

There is a limited amount anyone can do for the parents of a
child in the NICU. You can only send over so many casseroles, pray
so many prayers, stay up with them so many nights. Then the
demands of your own life take over again, and you can do little
more than wish them well and check in from time to time.

As the intensive phase of outside support slowly fades, parents
of the NICU frequently make connections with other parents—
especially the mothers.

Jewel quickly found Tracey Hagman. Tracey was a veteran of the
unit, having already been there seven weeks with her son, Simon.
When a new relationship is formed in the NICU, the veterans tend
to train the newcomers. They explain about the ventilators, eye
exams, brain scans, lung medications and so on. These are the
things to expect in this order. "They had already traveled,"
Anthony said, "where we were about to go."

The veterans are also evidence that you can make it. Someone
else has been down this path, and they are still here fighting, so
maybe things will work out for us as well.

But most important for Jewel, Tracey was a fellow believer. Here
was someone who shared her core convictions, who understood
that God was more important in this process than medical school

diplomas. "Tracey and I could always talk openly about God, and I knew she wouldn't think, *Oh yow*. It was a good feeling."

The relationship was cemented when after a week or so Tracey gave Lamarre one of Simon's big dinosaur balloons. Lamarre was about to have his first major surgery, and Tracey said it was his good luck dinosaur balloon. The Fosters, of course, don't believe in luck, but they do recognize good will and faith coming from others. They knew it was Tracey's way of saying, "We want God's best for you and Lamarre."

The Fosters not only want God's best, they expect it, maybe even insist on it—the way you insist on someone keeping his or her promise. They believe one way you ensure the fulfillment of that promise is to speak the promise out loud. You say what you want, what you expect, what you are patiently waiting for to come into being.

It's a strange belief to many. We create reality with our words. Maybe, when you consider the effect of encouraging or destructive words on the lives of children, it's not so strange.

But words affecting weight?

Weighing twenty ounces at birth, Lamarre was tiny even in a place where tiny is the norm. You have to see a human being this size before you can comprehend it. A father's wedding band slips over the fist and onto the arm like a large, dangling bracelet. Lamarre's head was slightly larger than a tennis ball.

But for Jewel, to talk about Lamarre's tinyness was to cooperate with death. "In the very beginning we would confess out of our mouths and say how big Lamarre was. The nurses would hand Lamarre to us out of the isolette and I'd go, 'Ah, he's so heavy!' and they'd say, 'Yeah, right.' But I'd say that kind of thing continuously, and then they start seeing him grow, and they'd be like, 'Whoa! He *is* getting big.'"

Jewel made it a point to talk about how much weight Lamarre was gaining to anyone in the area, including other mothers. She wanted that idea planted and growing up around Lamarre like grass

even when she wasn't there. One day another mother reported to
Jewel that she was sitting nearby with her own child when someone
walked by with a nurse and said, "My, that one is really small."

Lamarre and Anthony Foster

"No," the nurse contradicted her, "that's Lamarre. Lamarre is
heavy. He's getting bigger every day."

Sometimes NICU relationships between parents mask an
unstated rivalry. Who is winning and who is losing in the race
against death, the race against handicaps and abnormalities?
Everyone wants everyone else's kid to do well, to beat the odds. But
there are the rock-hard statistics that tell you that some will and
some won't. It's hard not to feel some envy when someone else's kid
is making progress and yours seems not to be.

The Fosters do not see it that way. Jewel says, "When people tell

me how well their new baby is doing, it just tells me that God
brought that person to me to let me know, 'Now do you think I care
more about this baby than I care about your baby? I care for all the
babies. It's just, Jewel, that you have to wait.' It's just a matter of
timing. They are coming into my path to help me understand what
God is going to do on behalf of Lamarre."

Anthony adds, with Jewel amening in the background, "I see
these people leaving for home with their babies and I say, 'One day,
that's going to be us.' It's as simple as that. 'That's going to be us,
packing up the area, excited, carrying balloons, and we're going to
be rolling Lamarre home.' "

People this positive about life's difficulties should either be committed to asylums or put in charge of the world.

They have an equally positive attitude about the hospital, a place
many long never to have to see again. Anthony says, "The hospital
is not a prison. This place is here to get you well and then they send
you home."

In fact, the Fosters view their endless time in the hospital not as
something pulling them away from normal or real life, but as what
their life was supposed to be right then—even as their calling.

"This is where God wanted me," Jewel says. "It's not about
Anthony and me, it's about Lamarre. God chose us to oversee
Lamarre, to be in charge of this child here on earth. We were leaving out the hospital one day and a woman said she had seen us frequently and asked if we worked at the hospital. And I said, 'Yes.'
And she asked where we worked. And I said, 'In the NICU.' She said
she thought she had seen us over there and asked us what we did
there. And I said, 'We're handling the Lord's business.' And she
looked at me kind of strange, and I said, 'We have a baby over there
that the Lord has put us in charge of and so we're handling his business.' And Anthony and I walked away, and we were laughing."

People frequently asked Jewel when she was going back to work.
The question started to bother her, so, as usual, she asked God
about it. "I say, 'Well, God? You know they're always asking when

I'm going back to work.' God says, 'You tell them that you're working.' So the next time the nurse asks when I'm going back to work, I
say 'Oh, I'm working.' And she's kind of surprised and asks, 'What
do you do?' And I say, 'Lamarre is my job.' "

The Fosters don't think of the months in the NICU as an afflic-
tion, either for themselves or for Lamarre. It was the place they
were called to be, for a season, for a purpose. When that season and
purpose were completed, they would go home with Lamarre but not
before. Anthony says, "We were not going *through* something, we
were going *to* something. The storm on the Sea of Galilee was not
sent to sink the disciples but to test them. This storm we were going
through was not to sink us, it was to sanctify us."

Anthony goes on, "It comes down to your belief system and
whether it is strong enough to get you through something like this.
Are you going to believe God, or are you going to be reduced to
'knock on wood' and 'good luck' and 'what does my horoscope say
today?' "

Jewel adds, "You need to establish your faith in God *before* the
crisis hits. Develop it when there aren't any great problems. We
sought God when things were going well, and so we were ready for
difficult times. And this has not been an easy time. This experience
is a birthing for us. We've got to push this miracle through. We're
pushing to get this miracle accomplished."

Anthony picks up the metaphor.

"All this is the labor. With every birth, your joy comes at the end.
You've got to get through the nine months and the labor."

But of course the Fosters didn't get the full nine months. And
that was the problem. Or was it? Jewel offers an unusual way of
looking on the experience of having an extremely premature child:
"The forming of a child in the womb is a secret. God let me see the
secret at five months. That's a privilege. We get to see the last four
months that are usually kept secret. Not everybody gets in on the
secret. We are privileged and honored to be allowed to see this. It
may be a tragedy to others, but it is a privilege to me."

A privilege? Four months premature, twenty ounces, the possibility of brain damage, endless days in the NICU, the complete disruption of their lives, pain for Lamarre and for Jewel and Anthony? An honor?

But maybe we don't know enough to call it a "disruption" of life. Maybe this kind of experience is when we are closest to really being alive. Maybe we too quickly reject pain as always evil, always something to eliminate at any cost. Maybe.

Jewel and Anthony are not typical. They don't see the need to be.

The Fosters told Lamarre's story while he was still in the hospital. That great, going home day did finally arrive when Lamarre was ten months old. The boy with the list finally overcame each numbered obstacle, and Jewel and Anthony proudly took him home. We will hear of Lamarre again.

CHAPTER TWO

SIMON
A SLOW MIRACLE

"This shouldn't be."

SIMON'S DELIVERY DOCTOR

*"Therefore do not worry about tomorrow,
for tomorrow will worry about itself. Each
day has enough trouble of its own."*

MATTHEW 6:34*

I can't find a heartbeat."

These are not the words a young, pregnant mother wants to hear. In Tracey's case, it got worse from there.

"I think you've lost the baby. We're going to do a D & C, but I'm going to get an OB down here to make sure."

D & C stands for dilatation and curettage, a procedure to clean out the contents of a womb. In this case, the contents were Simon Hagman.

It took an hour to get the obstetrician. In the meantime Tracey and Eric contemplated the end of a two-month pregnancy and the end of their hopes for a brother or sister for their first child,

---

*This verse and italicized passages throughout this chapter appear in Tracey's journal.

Sammy. Then Eric made an announcement.

"The baby's not dead."

Tracey was not in the mood for hollow optimism.

"Yes, it is."

"No, God has told me the baby's not dead."

"No, he didn't."

It's not usually very fruitful to disagree with someone who believes God has told them something. But Tracey was too upset to do anything but grieve over the inevitable.

The obstetrician finally arrived and did an ultrasound.

"Well, there's the heartbeat."

Tracey felt like her own heart had stopped.

"You're not having a miscarriage. Your placenta is not fully attached to the side of the uterus, and so it leaks."

The only hope was complete bed rest for the remainder of the pregnancy. Perhaps the placenta would heal and the bleeding would stop.

But it never did.

"I bled every day for months. God brought to my mind the story in the New Testament where the woman has been bleeding for years and she touches Jesus' robe and she's healed. For the first time I identified with that woman, and I felt that God told me he was going to heal me, just like that woman. I didn't get a letter or hear an audible voice, but you know when the Holy Spirit sort of speaks to you."

Tracey believed God told her that not only was she going to be healed, but that her baby would be too. "I felt like it was going to be a big thing. There were going to be so many miracles, and God was just preparing me for it."

Her OB said she had to make it to twenty-five weeks' gestation or the baby wouldn't have a chance. Twenty-five was the magic number, the goal line, the Promised Land. Anything less would be too little too soon.

If twenty-five weeks was the minimum, twenty-two weeks was the fact. At twenty-two weeks Tracey began having contractions at home.

She went into the hospital and spent the night. In the morning the nurse came in to check her and announced, "Your water broke."

Hard on her heels was a doctor running in. He had a question.

"Do you want us to try to save the child?"

This is one version of what has become a standard question since the early 1970s: "Do you want this child?" A strange question really. "Do you want this child?" As though one was trying to decide whether or not to buy a new car. "Do you want this car, or is it the wrong color? Do you want this child, or is it the wrong time?" The unstated assumption is that the child has no value independent of your wanting it. It is either of ultimate value or utterly worthless depending on the degree to which you desire it.

Try asking it other ways and see how it sounds. "Does the thought of this child please you?" "Is this a convenient time for you?" "Does this child fit into your schedule?" Then put your own name in the sentence and imagine someone else asking the question about you. "Do you want _____?" "Is this a convenient time for _____?" "Does _____'s life fit into your schedule?" And if the answer is no?

Tracey was stunned by the question—"Do you want us to try to save this child?"—and repeated her one word answer over and over lest there be some misunderstanding of her desires.

"Yes, yes, yes, yes, yes!"

But it was a yes filled with despair. "We just started to cry because we knew he was twenty-two weeks, and there was no way he was going to make it." They were short of the goal line. A long run, a heroic effort, but no score and the game was over.

Tracey was taken by ambulance to Abbott-Northwestern Hospital. They managed to hold off delivery for five more days through the use of drugs, but then Simon's heart rate began to drop and the doctors decided they would have to take him out by caesarean section.

But as they were preparing her for the C-section, Tracey announced, "It's coming out." And come out he did, all twenty ounces and twelve and one-half inches of him. The delivering doctor said, somewhat cryptically, "This shouldn't be."

Tracey and Eric didn't know exactly how to act. Eric did the male thing. Or at least *a* male thing. He made jokes. He was acting happy, thinking that was how he was supposed to act.

Eric's jokes made Tracey angry. "I thought, *What are you doing?* I was feeling grief. I wasn't feeling any joy. I was feeling grief and pain, and here he was running around making jokes. It was very scary. I didn't know if our baby would live another hour."

The medical staff didn't give them any false hopes. The delivery had come at two in the morning. They said to Tracey as she was taken to a recovery room, "We'll call you tonight . . . if anything happens." His chances of making it through the first night were not good.

But then the medical people didn't factor in the prayer chains. How could they?

I call on you, O God, for you will answer me; give ear to me and hear my prayer. Show the wonder of your great love, you who save by your right hand. (Psalm 17:6-7)

"We had some prayer chains already prepared," Tracey remembers, "so we called when I went into labor, and I'd say about 150 people were praying immediately." Tracey called the three key prayer-chain people, and they called others, and within minutes many people were praying in agreement with Tracey and Eric for the life of their child. You don't need to have figured out exactly how prayer works to know that this is a good thing.

Be joyful always; pray continually; give thanks in all circumstances. (1 Thessalonians 5:16-18)

Simon changed how Eric thinks of prayer.

"I have seen prayer in action, and I believe more in . . . I don't want to say changing God's mind, but in pleading with him for our heart's desire. We wanted Simon to live no matter what he might be like or not like. And we feel confidence in coming before the Lord and asking him for that, whereas before I might just pray, 'Whatever your will is God, amen.'"

*   *   *

Six hours after delivery they met Dr. Hoekstra for the first time. The immediate concerns were bleeding in the brain and the condition of Simon's heart. Dr. Hoekstra reassured them the best he could but said somewhat ominously, "If his brain bleeds, I'll tell you what I think."

Simon had his first test for bleeding in the brain on his third day of life. There was no sign of bleeding so far, but there are many weeks to go. Not all the bad things that can happen to preemies happen at the beginning. It is not a smooth ascent from danger to safety, from hurt to healing. There is trouble enough for each day, and trouble is nothing if not patient.

Simon's heart, for instance. The blood vessel connecting the two main arteries that closes spontaneously in full-term babies was still open, threatening his blood pressure and his lungs. He was given medication during the first three days of life, but it had not worked, and surgery, always risky for a baby born at twenty-two weeks, seemed inevitable.

Tracey and Eric, however, are not servants to the inevitable.

Over the first weeks of Simon's life, they became cultivators of rare events. "We sent out prayer letters once a month," Tracey recalls, "that had specific medical information on what to pray for. So we immediately, that day, sent out a letter asking people to pray for three things—no brain bleed, the blood vessel to close and for his skin to heal. His brain didn't bleed, he never had one skin breakdown, and I was there when they did the echocardiogram of his heart. The guy looked at me and said, 'I don't believe it. The vessel has closed.'"

> *Then you will know that I am the Lord; those who hope in me will not be disappointed. (Isaiah 49:23)*

Praying parents and dedicated doctors working to save the fragile life of a beautiful, tiny baby . . . makes a great movie scene. But there are many times when even parents of great faith wouldn't want their thoughts and actions put up on a screen for others to judge. And it takes a lot of honesty and perhaps the desire to help others to admit it.

Take for instance how Tracey felt at first when she looked at Simon.

"One thing I really struggled with was guilt when Simon was born, because I didn't want to look at him or touch him because he looked so . . . well, gross."

Eric chimes in. "He looked so . . . unbabylike. Not like your image of how a baby should look."

And she continues, "His skin was so see-through that he looked like he had a sunburn. So bright red. So premature his eyes were still fused shut, like a kitten."

Perhaps in the background of this reaction lay fear of bonding to a seemingly doomed child. Why get too close to someone who, at any moment, is going to break your heart? And then there were all the machines and tubes. Even the small strips of tape holding the endotracheal tube in place covered much of his face. This was no Gerber baby, and the natural maternal instincts were momentarily deflected.

But only momentarily.

"A couple of days after he was born, I shared my feelings in tears with a friend. And she said to me, 'Tracey, you can't. You have to interact with him, because if the Lord decides to take him, you'll be so upset.' And it just clicked. I said, 'You're right. What am I thinking?' So five minutes later I was down there, touching him. I put my hand in the isolette, and I touched his hand, and I just looked at him. And, you know, he was beautiful."

As the heavens are higher than the earth, so are my ways higher than your ways and my thoughts than your thoughts. (Isaiah 55:9)

Simon's brain scans continued to reveal no bleeding, and the echocardiogram showed the vessel connecting the arteries had closed properly. He was stabilized and doing well. Then suddenly he wasn't doing well at all. It was time for one of the phone calls from the hospital that Tracey hated.

"It's those phone calls that you get. In the first few weeks every call gives you a heart attack. 'You have to come down right now,' they say. 'You have to come immediately.' We had two of those, and the second was the worse. I was out, and they couldn't get a hold of me. I finally got home, and there are all these messages on the machine. So I call, and Dr. Vicksburg says, 'Tracey, Simon is very sick. You need to come down here right now.'

"I got off the phone, and I just started to bawl. I was standing there crying, and Sammy, who was three, started crying because he saw that I was upset, and he didn't know what was happening.

"So my mother-in-law came over to take care of Sammy, and I walked out the door. I was driving to the hospital, and I was just screaming at God because I didn't know if Simon was going to be alive when I got there. And I said, 'God, I don't feel your peace. You promised me your peace, and I don't feel it. You promised! I don't feel peace at all. I don't feel it at all. Don't do this to me!'

"All of a sudden, I just slumped in my car. It was like the Holy Spirit just went 'whoosh.' I was totally calm, almost like in a trance. It was definitely God. He just overcame me."

Do not be anxious about anything, but in everything by prayer and petition, with thanksgiving, present your requests to God. And the peace of God, which transcends all understanding, will guard your hearts and minds in Christ Jesus. (Philippians 4:6-7)

Being overcome by God is something you remember. But the feeling doesn't necessarily last a long time.

"I felt peace, and I was able to drive to the hospital. And when I got down there and walked into the room, all the doctors were standing around Simon's isolette, and I started to hyperventilate. I started taking my eyes off the Lord and just started hyperventilating. They sat me down and said, 'We're not sure if he's going to make it.'"

The apostle Peter comes to mind. Jesus is walking on the water, and impetuous Peter wants to walk on the water too. So he joins Jesus in this highly unscientific adventure, and what do you know, he *is* walking on water. And apparently his thinking goes something like this: *I'm doing it! I'm doing it! I'm walking on the water with Jesus. I'm doing it! I'm . . . what am I doing? What am I doing? How am I doing it? I'm sinking! I'm going to drown!*

Not all of that is reported in the Bible, of course, but perhaps it's close. It's also close to what Tracey experienced, and it grows out of that persistent and recurring gap between promise and fulfillment, petition and realization, things hoped for and things seen.

"God had told Eric way back when we were two months pregnant that Simon was going to live and that Eric was going to see grandchildren through Simon, and he had given us all these Bible verses, and here they were telling us that maybe Simon wasn't going to make it."

God seemed to say *this*, yet now we are seeing *that*. The Bible promises *x*, but I am experiencing *y*. The life of faith requires putting *x* and *y* together in a way that retains both the sovereignty and power and goodness of God, and the undeniable reality of what's in front of my nose.

So Tracey had a question for Eric, one that she asked over and over through tears. "Is God still telling you that Simon is going to live? Is God still telling you that Simon is going to live?"

It's not the first time someone has tried to draw comfort from someone else's faith when her own was sapped.

Eric said, "Yes. God is still telling me that."

That would have to do.

When I am afraid, I will trust in you. (Psalm 56:3)

Because of worsening lung disease, they put Simon on a high frequency ventilator that gave him 420 breaths of oxygen per minute, seven every second. It appears to be a harsh, even violent treatment, causing Simon's purse-sized body to vibrate with each burst.

He made it through that day, but the next day part of his right lung collapsed. Furthermore, the rest of the right lung and his entire left lung were overexpanded and trapping air, giving them a cystlike appearance on the x-ray.

The standard procedure for treating such a problem is to put the baby on its side in hopes the overexpansion dissipates on its own. But because both lungs were involved and one was partially collapsed, that wasn't possible.

Tracey and Eric sent word out to the prayer chains to pray specifically that the cystlike condition would resolve itself. At the same time, Tracey began fasting in hopes that Simon would get off the high frequency ventilator. "It's so hard to watch your baby shaking."

But Dr. Hoekstra was not encouraging on that score.

There's no way I'm taking Simon off it today. We tried it yesterday, and it didn't work. He needs it for a couple of more days."

Trust in the LORD with all your heart and lean not on your own understanding; in all your ways acknowledge him, and he will make your paths straight. (Proverbs 3:5-6)

Tracey left the unit to work through a few things in her mind.

"I said I was going to be gone for a couple of hours. I was depressed. I went outside, and God kept saying, 'Do you trust me? Do you trust me? Do you trust me?' And I just didn't know if I did. I mean, I did trust him, but here Dr. Hoekstra had just said he wasn't going to get off the high frequency ventilator today."

After a couple of hours outside the hospital she turned and marched back in with a rather strange prayer in her heart.

"Lord, if Simon is not off that ventilator, I can't go back in there today, because I can't deal with it. So please turn me around. Have me bump into someone—or something—because I can't function anymore today with him like that.

"And God kept saying, 'Just keep on walking.' And I said five times, if not ten, 'God, please, only if he's not on the ventilator.

Please turn me around. Please. I can't go back in there. I can't! I
can't.' And I remember the doors opening to the unit, and it was the
biggest leap of faith because Dr. Hoekstra had said there's no way
he'd be off the ventilator, and yet I had fasted. And I walked down
that long hallway and into the unit, and there was Simon, and he
was off the high frequency ventilator and doing ten times better
than when I left. And I just had this glow! I just broke out in this
huge smile because no one knew what had just happened. It was a
big thing, you know."

*With man this is impossible, but not with God; all things are possi-
ble with God. (Mark 10:27)*

Yes, a big thing. In a long series of big things. Surrounded by
countless little things—many of which were hard to understand,
much less explain to someone else. And, by the way, an x-ray that
same day showed that the cystlike condition had disappeared.

Would Simon have been off the high frequency ventilator without the prayer? Would the lungs have cleared up anyway? There's
no scientific test for such questions because we only get one try at
each moment of our lives. We can't try dealing with a certain condition with prayer and then without prayer to see which one works
better because, though patterns may recur, the train of time moves
steadily down the track. Life offers no retakes.

So, with some situations in life, you pray—maybe even if you
don't believe in it. You pray as best you can, for as long as there is
hope. Because there is precious little else you can do. Praying
becomes your main job.

Slowly Tracey and Eric begin to see this job differently than they
did at first. Early on, they moved from praying for God's will, whatever that might be, to praying for their own heart's desire—that
Simon be healed. They also moved from praying generally, "Please
make Simon better," to praying very specifically, "Lord, stop those
capillaries from growing in his eyes so that Simon does not lose his
sight." Not that God didn't know about those capillaries, but that he

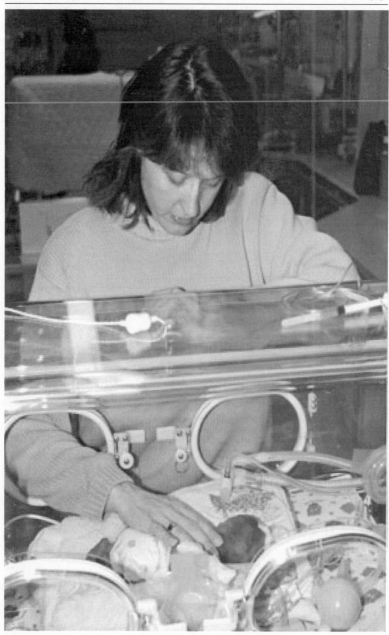

Tracey Hagman comforts one-week-old Simon in his isolette

tells us to ask for what we want. And there seems to be something about the *asking*, in faith, that releases the power to make it happen.

It was believing this that took them to the next step—believing that something *had* happened before there was any visible confirmation that it had. Tracey came upon Hebrews 11:1, and she grabbed it with both hands: "Now faith is being sure of what we hope for and certain of what we do not see."

"When Simon's lung collapsed and all this happened, I was beside myself with frustration and grief and terror. And God brought me a verse that says faith is not what you see but what you hope for. And I said, 'Yes, that's it. I can't see it, but I've got to believe it.' It was a novel idea to me, and it changed my whole attitude that day. They were telling me his lung had collapsed, and Eric turned to me and said, 'You're so peaceful,' and I said, 'God's shown me that I have hope. It doesn't matter what I'm seeing.'"

He saved us, not because of righteous things we had done, but because of his mercy. (Titus 3:5)

If there wasn't this tension between what is promised and what we see, it wouldn't be faith and it wouldn't be real. As Tracey relates the memory of God's revelation to her—"God's shown me that I have hope. It doesn't matter what I'm seeing"—she adds, "And yet, that's so hard when it's your kid and you question it constantly."

Yes, it's so hard when it's your kid. All of the aspects of the life of faith—the commands, the expectations, the admonitions, the encouragements—are perfectly acceptable, even attractive, in the abstract, but often "so hard" in the living. And in this case the life on the line is your child's, and he has a name—Simon—and a brother—Sammy—and parents—Eric and Tracey—and grandparents—James and Milly, Joel and Marylee—whose hearts will break if he doesn't make it, and there is no guarantee that the next hour will not be his last.

And so we "question it constantly" *even as* we are believing and obeying. It is not one or the other, believing or questioning, it is both at the same time. "I do believe," says the man pleading to Jesus for the life of his son in the Gospel of Mark, and in the same breath he whispers, "Help me overcome my unbelief." If you think doubt cancels out belief or that belief cancels out doubt, then you probably have never stared at twenty ounces of your own flesh and blood struggling to live.

In dancing with faith and doubt, one hopes not to dance alone. God is in the dance, but so are other human dancers. Tracey is blessed with a good husband and a greatly supportive family. But even good husbands are sometimes not what women wish them to be.

They sometimes don't seem to adequately share the grief, the worry, the "what's going to be become of us" of the whole experience. It's not that men don't feel it; it's that men often don't demonstrate it. They bypass the external clues, verbal and nonverbal, that women give to each other and to anyone within two city blocks that say, "Something important is happening here, and I need to touch or talk about it, and preferably both."

And when men are perceived as not sharing all this, they can be perceived as indifferent to it. Tracey didn't like it when Eric made jokes at Simon's birth. She also didn't like it when he shut up.

During the third week of Simon's life, Tracey wrote in her journal to Simon, *"This is hard. . . . Daddy and I feel different emotions. I want him to feel the same way I do—overwhelmed, consumed, helpless. He seems to feel much more peaceful and trusting. Now I think his faith is greater than mine at times. How can he be so peaceful when all of this is going on?"*

The generous impulse is to credit Eric with greater faith. The nagging suspicion is that he, like most men, simply doesn't get it. "We are having this life-threatening crisis here, buddy, and you are humming along like we're watching the Super Bowl half-time show." Women want and need people to react to what's happening, to register it in some appropriate way.

They want compassion in the most fundamental sense. The word *compassion* literally means "to suffer with." A compassionate person takes on the grief of the other as her own. The lines that separate one person from another are blurred, and for the moment at least, the burden is shared and therefore more bearable.

What Tracey seemed to get from Eric instead of compassion was strength—a good thing but not the only needed thing. And therefore what he got back from her was frustration and judgment. "I couldn't understand how Simon could have a cardiac arrest and almost die, and five hours later Eric would go to work." If you are the mother of a gravely sick child, there should not be any such thing as "work"—or, for that matter, grocery shopping, sporting events, politics, the evening news, insurance forms, chatty phone calls or vacuum tracks in your carpet before company comes. The world should close down, hold its breath, pay attention. For, you see, my child is on the edge of death.

No temptation has seized you except what is common to man. And God is faithful; he will not let you be tempted beyond what you can bear. (1 Corinthians 10:13)

*   *   *

In addition to spouses and family, a potential source of strength and comfort are the equally tiny, equally threatened babies in the surrounding isolettes—and their parents.

An unwritten rule in the NICU is that parents pay attention to their own child and do not intrude on the privacy of other parents and infants. There are so many difficult stories crowded into such a relatively small area that the fiction of privacy is maintained to create the psychological and spiritual space needed to focus on one's vigil. The rule is stay to yourself. Fortunately, it is often broken.

Most mothers cannot stand day after day over their children in plastic arks, fifteen feet from mothers on either side standing over their babies in their plastic arks, without eventually breaking a few rules. The one thing every parent of a severely premature baby has is a story, and stories require someone to share them with.

The journal Tracey kept during the first five months of Simon's life records traces of four other life stories that intertwined with her son's. The first reference in the journal to other children in the unit comes when Simon is almost a month old. Up to this point there has not been time or energy to look to the right or the left.

One of those was a tiny boy whom Tracey saw as a trailblazer, though she hoped Simon wouldn't have to follow exactly the same difficult path.

There is another little boy, Burgess, right by you. He has been in the hospital for seven months. I'm also praying for him. I selfishly hope that you won't go through any of that. Oh Simon, we just don't know. God gives us answers for just today.

The next day Tracey writes more to Simon about the boy everyone will come to call B. J.

His parents are from Liberia. He has been in the NICU for seven months. He has had many problems but lots of miracles. . . . Today they will try a medicine on him as a last hope to get the blood pressure in his lungs to go down. His mother and I prayed for a long time last night for both of you. She anointed you with oil. Today I am fasting for you and Burgess. We are praying for victory today for Burgess—victory today for Simon. Victory that only comes by Jesus.

And then one day there is a journal entry about another boy we already know.

There is a new little boy who has come to join us. His name is Lamarre. He is twenty-two weeks and one pound, four ounces. Oh precious God, I ask that you would save Lamarre's life so that he could honor and praise you. You are so good to us, God. We ask that you would help out Lamarre.

Parents conduct campaigns for the lives of their children. In addition to organizing the prayer chains, Tracey had "Please Pray for Simon" buttons made with his picture on them. She passed

them out like a political organizer. And she posted a sign in the window of their home that said, "Mighty is our God! Hurray for
Simon!" This is a woman who does not seem to care that religion,
in our society, is supposed to be polite and private.

She also risks being considered a pain in the neck by the doctors
and nurses. Like many mothers in her situation, she becomes an
overnight expert on her child's ailments, and she uses that knowledge, such as it is, to ensure that he gets optimal care. "I'm like his
advocate in the hospital. I'm an advocate for my child. I talk to the
doctors. I read the charts. I'm sort of like the stalker. I'm addicted
to the facts. Someone in each family usually becomes that way."

It is no surprise, then, that a natural campaigner like Tracey will
recruit other mothers into Simon's battle for life and that she will
try to fight as hard for their children as she does for her own. So
B. J.'s mother follows the New Testament prescription and anoints
Simon's head with oil. And Tracey fasts for Burgess. And the goal is
victory—victory over despair, victory over high blood pressure, victory over death. Through Jesus.

But prayer chains and buttons and window signs and monitoring
medical charts and fervent prayer don't necessarily spell the end of
questioning and doubt. There is a pattern that runs throughout
Tracey's journal: encouragement and faith are followed by sadness
and questioning, and then again by hopefulness. These are the various faces of faith.

The day after anointing and fasting for victory comes an honest
admission.

> *My faith wavers so much, Simon. I believe one minute and not the
> next. I'm learning so much about faith. Burgess's mom has some
> serious faith. She has believed Burgess would live through all of his
> major problems. Simon, I want that kind of faith. I have it at times.
> I love you and want you to come home.*

It is healthy, when one's own faith has slowed to a trickle, to join
it with a larger flow. Faith refreshes faith when two or more are

gathered together, and it can even give rise to thoughts of travel.

Wednesday night there are a few women from the NICU who are going to get together to pray for our children. Two of the ladies are from Africa originally. Africa is always in my heart and soul. I hope one day you will be able to go to Africa with me and see how beautiful it is.

Tracey had spent time in Africa before she was married. And if it is pleasant for her to picture herself someday traveling back to Africa with Simon, then it is even more pleasant, a week later, to envision two very fragile infants someday being friends. *"We pray for each other's babies always. B. J.'s mom lives very close to us. We talk about you and B. J. being good friends one day."*

A severely premature birth sends ripples of influence and reaction radiating far beyond those at the center. Help comes not only from spouses and family and friends and staff; it comes also from those one has never seen and may never even hear about.

It might even come from China.

One thing about prayer chains is that you never know if and where they are going to stop. Link leads to link, which spawns collateral links that even those a link or two away are not aware of. They can lead around the world—and beyond the world.

"I run into people all the time who say, 'Oh, you're Simon's mom. I've been praying for you for two years.' That just makes me want to cry every time."

We have a special place in our hearts for people who genuinely love our children, especially people who don't have to—and even more especially people who have never met them and yet beseech heaven on their behalf.

"I am constantly meeting people I don't know who will turn to the person with them and say, 'This is Simon's mother, the baby we're praying for in the Bible study.' One mother introduced me to her six-year-old son, and the boy told me his kindergarten class prayed for Simon every day last year. And I don't even know how they knew about Simon. It's very humbling."

Humbling because in an individualistic society like ours, with its emphasis on self-sufficiency, it is humbling to feel helpless and to receive the help, often unsolicited, of others. Humbling also, perhaps, to call and enlist others to call on the God of the universe to turn his ear to your pleas for your child in this tiny bed at this moment.

An anthropomorphic way of conceiving it, yes. But also a biblical one. The psalmist and the prophets call on God to lean down from heaven, to look and see, to listen, please, to what is weighing on me now, to attend to my pain, to respond to my need. If it is anthropomorphic—in the shape of humans—it is because we are, in fact, only human, and God seems willing to meet us as we are.

> Praise the LORD, O my soul, and forget not all his benefits—who forgives all your sins and heals all your diseases. (Psalm 103:2-3)

Back to China.

"We got a call from a friend a couple of weeks ago whose sister was in China doing missions and was talking to these other missionaries. They started talking about this Simon they had been praying for. And this friend's sister had been praying for Simon too, and so here some people meet in China who don't even know each other, and they find that they both are praying for the same child who neither of them have ever seen."

A sister of a friend, who meets someone in China, who . . . Not a miracle, really. But perhaps not a coincidence either. Rather, another bit of evidence that encourages the belief that we live in a providential world—a world where things connect, where there is a link between act and consequence—a world where prayer matters.

Or, as Tracey puts it, "It's huge—just the fact that Simon has brought people to their knees—hundreds and hundreds of people. And God loves it when his people pray."

Yes, lots of support and lots of prayer. And Simon was going to need every bit of it. For Simon wasn't a one-miracle, one-prayer baby. He had an appetite for crisis that appeared at times to be a hunger for death.

In November of 1996 Tracey went into the hospital for a normal visit. Simon had graduated out of the NICU to the PICU, the pediatric intensive care unit. He was still having problems getting enough oxygen, and his appetite wasn't what it should be, but Tracey felt he was making progress, and there was no sign of anything unusual. On this day, however, Simon taught them a lesson that is reinforced time and again for those born too soon—progress today is no guarantee against disaster tomorrow.

"I walked into the unit for a normal visit, and I saw all the doors strewn open in his room, and the code red light was going off, and the doctor was doing chest compressions on him." Simon was having cardiac arrest.

"And I walked in there, and the nurse saw me and grabbed my arm to stop me and said, 'Mrs. Hagman . . .' and I said, 'Let go of my arm!' Because I knew immediately I had to go in there and lay hands on my son and pray. I mean I just knew.

"And so I walked in, and I didn't know if he was dead or alive because he was limp. He was just lying there. And the doctor that was working on him was a Christian, and she accepts me.

"And I lay hands on Simon to pray, and what came out of my mouth was 'In the name of Jesus Christ, Satan, I rebuke you. You cannot have my son's life, and I command you to leave this room—now!'"

Wrestling with Satan over the life of your child. No wonder the concerns of everyday life pale and fade away. Once you have found yourself giving orders to Satan, you have a diminished tolerance for the trivial.

But after such a jarring experience, Tracey is tempted to wonder in retrospect what, in fact, really happened. "I don't know if it was my prayers or the people that were praying or what, but Simon was stabilized. And of course after I had prayed and done all that, I left the room and had a nervous breakdown. But I had done my duty."

Done her duty indeed. There is quite a bit of duty in all this.

Quite a bit of putting in the hours and doing all the things that have
to be done because, for this season of your life, that is the job you
have been given to do. Not a job you ever applied for but one you
have been given nonetheless. And some days you even see that it is,
in fact, just that—a gift.

Other days it's just an exhausting, soul-sapping, brain-numbing
load. There's a little drumbeat in the background of all that Tracey
describes—Eric too, but mostly Tracey—a little drumbeat behind the
trumpet blasts of miracle and the sweet strings of grace. It is the
drumbeat of weariness. She doesn't complain about it. It's just always
there, as it is for the parents of every severely premature baby.

Oh Simon, this is such a roller coaster—Mommy is so tired emo-
tionally and physically.

And that entry came at the two-week mark, when the tiredness
was new, even superficial. In time, tiredness becomes institutional-
ized, a numbing haze covering everything like brown urban smog.
Five weeks later the expression of fatigue sounds almost biblical.
"Oh dear Lord I am so tired." It is a groan too deep for words. And
yet it leads to more words, as though Tracey is afraid that express-
ing her tiredness will be mistaken for ingratitude or lack of faith.

"But God, I do know you are in control. You have to be. God—
without you I have no hope. Give me the faith to trust you with my
son's life." And then she claims a promise, something Tracey does
on almost every page of her journal: *"Whatever you ask for in*
prayer, believe that you have received it, and it will be yours
(Mark 11:24)."

Having a child like Simon often leads to some heavy bargaining
with God. Tracey is not above using a psalm to remind God that
perhaps he himself will benefit from a life spared: *"Turn O LORD*
and deliver me; save me because of your unfailing love. No one
remembers you when he is dead. Who praises you from the grave?
(Psalm 6:4-5)."

Tiredness is especially hard to bear when there seems to be no progress. We don't mind feeling tired at the end of the day if we think our exertions have accomplished something. I am exhausted, but there is a pile of split wood, a stack of processed papers or a clean house to show for it. But what if, at the end of the day—or the night—there is a very sick child who is no better than yesterday, perhaps worse?

> *I'm starting to get so tired of the up and down of being at the NICU. I want to see great progress with you every day, and that's just not the way it seems to go. It's two steps forward, one step back. Oh Lord, I need to have hope just from you, oh my God. My soul is tired. I need to see progress. If I can't, please give me the faith to trust you. "I will take refuge in the shadow of your wings until the disaster has passed" (Psalm 57:1).*

It is a real question whether the disaster will, in fact, ever pass. Perhaps it will only *arrive* in full. Or perhaps it will never really either arrive, with the death of your child, or pass, with your child certified healthy and whole. Perhaps it will be crisis, followed by progress, followed by new crisis, followed by decline, followed by neither progress nor decline, ad infinitum.

With Simon, for instance, the next step on the path was another cardiac arrest. It is November, and the doctors have made an incision in Simon's throat for the placement of a tracheostomy. He is connected to a ventilator that will help his body get enough oxygen, something his lungs haven't been able to manage on their own. It is progress over having a tube in his mouth or nose, because now he can suck, swallow and smile, and do other normal baby things. But how good can you feel about the prospect of your child breathing through a hole in his throat for the next year or two?

Still, the doctors are talking about Simon maybe coming home in a month or two, perhaps after Christmas. It's not to be. In early December Tracey gets one of those calls. Simon is having another cardiac arrest. He survives it, but they spend his first Christmas in intensive care.

And Simon's second arrest is simply a warm-up for his third. As he recovers from the December cardiac arrest, Tracey and Eric work on getting the house ready for his coming home. They add a bathroom for the nursing staff that will be in their home at all hours and try to arrange things so they can have a little privacy when, in a sense, the hospital comes to them.

Simon is supposed to come home February 28. They are nervous but also expectant. The day of coming home from the hospital is often fervently, if naively, wished for like the day of release from a concentration camp. It has, in anticipation, the feel of victory and freedom and return to the long-lamented "normal life." That the reality is often different does not matter in Simon's case, because the day of release turns into the day of disaster.

"We got a phone call that said please come down to the hospital, your son's having another cardiac arrest. So we went down and this was the worst one. I walked in and again there were a million doctors in there, and they were shaking their heads at me and saying, 'I don't think he's going to live.' And we went in the backroom and just prayed and were very upset and emotional. The seventh time—this would be the seventh time in a year that someone said, 'Your son is going to die,' and each time you go through that emotion of death. It's so painful. From the first time I went into the emergency room early in my pregnancy they said he was dead. He's always been told he's dead."

On that first occasion Eric had said, "No, he isn't dead." He had been right, and Tracey always took a lot of comfort in her husband's conviction and strength. But this time it wasn't there. This time Eric believed the facts as they were presented to him. And Tracey, who has always wanted more emotion out of Eric, didn't like it when she saw it.

"I knew things were bad when Eric came into the room and just freaked out. I remember he was kicking the wall, and he said, 'My son is going to die!' And I thought, *Oh my gosh! Things are bad because my husband's losing it.* And I remember I grabbed him

and said, 'If he's going to die, we have to go back in there and be
with him. We can't sit in this room and scream.' So we walked back
in, and we were praying and laying our hands on him and asking
the Lord to spare his life. We called our pastors all to come down
and lay hands on him. You know, there's no right way to do it."

Yes, there is no right way to do it. No single right way. No invari-
able script. No clear map. Just do what you can do and gather the
forces of the universe the best you can and wait.

And, while you wait, deal with questions that make no sense to
you. Like this one from a doctor they greatly respected who, in the
middle of Simon's cardiac arrest, asked, "If he has another arrest,
do you want us just to let him go?"

Hadn't they heard this question before? "Do you want us to try
to save the child?" The answer then had been "Yes, yes, yes, yes,
yes!" It was the same now, only with a different word.

"No, we don't want you to let him go. Yesterday we were worrying about his having an ear infection, and today you want to know if
you should let him go."

Tracey and Eric were incredulous at the question, but the doctor
had her reasons. Simon was "code red" for four hours. A team of
doctors and nurses worked on him constantly. But in the end he
once again survived. There was obvious concern about how long an
adequate flow of oxygen to his brain may have been compromised,
but he appeared all right. "They said it was the worst arrest they
had ever seen a child survive."

*   *   *

Year one: three cardiac arrests, chronic lung disease, pulmonary
hypertension, potential blindness, failed hearing tests and contin-
ual threats to most of his major systems. Not to mention the garden-variety crises, continuous tests, constant interventions and
numberless procedures. Add the phone calls, care conferences,
insurance forms, drives to and from the hospital. Consider also

arranging babysitters, informing the prayer chains, writing letters, cleaning the house, doing laundry and making meals. At the same time, *if* there is time, try being a wife or husband, a friend and perhaps someone with a full-time job.

It is no wonder that Tracey at times would like to be a little girl again, no wonder that she yearns for someone more powerful than she to fix things, to make everything okay. And it is understandable that this is how she sometimes sees God, our *Abba* Father.

"God wants to do things for us just like I want to do things for my kids. God loves me so much more than I love my kids. And God . . . God's our dad. And I know that the last time Simon had a cardiac arrest, I did all the right praying. I had rebuked Satan, and I had claimed Scripture, and I had prayed with my husband and all the things you are supposed to do, and things were not getting better. And I remember falling on my knees in tears and saying to God, 'You are my dad. Dads fix things. Daddies fix things.' My dad fixed things when I was growing up. He fixed things for me. Daddies are supposed to fix. And it was such a revelation to me that it was that simple. 'Please fix it.' And he did."

Unless you have the faith of a child, the Bible says, you will not see the kingdom of God. This is literally childlike faith—simple and profound. Childlike, not childish. But even this kind of faith is tempered with adult experience when Tracey adds, "But he doesn't always fix it the way we want."

*   *   *

It would be a serious distortion to depict the first year of Simon's life as only stress, calamity, anxiety and scrapes with death. As well as the joy that comes from shared faith and the simple wonder of new life, there was a string of small victories that perhaps only those who have experienced it can understand.

Such as seeing your child's nose for the first time. A premature

baby is so tiny that a couple of pieces of tape holding the endotracheal tube can cover much of the face. At ten days of Simon's life,
Tracey gets a partial view.

*I was able to see more of your nose last night. It's the cutest nose
I've ever seen. Last night was the first time I really experienced joy
with you. I've been so emotional and worried—last night you were
responding to me so much. You love when I give you water on a Q-
Tip. I'm dying to see your face better.*

Any sign that the child is aware of you is cherished. The eyes of
these children are initially tightly closed. Their bodies are not yet
prepared to interact with their surroundings. They do not kick
their legs or wave their arms or do what we think of as baby
things. They were designed to still have months within the womb,
and their whole being is occupied in a silent, near motionless contest for life. So the slightest suggestion of interaction brings joy to
a mother's heart.

*Today you liked it when I held your hand. You squeezed back, and it
was wonderful.*

That at three weeks. And then at four, the joy of finger sucking.

*Last night I held your fingers up to your mouth so you could suck
them. You kind of were sucking on my finger too. I was in heaven.*

Only when the trivial things of life have been stripped away by
the prospect of death do we appropriately value the act of a baby
sucking on our finger.

*This afternoon I was so excited to hear you making a sucking
noise while your fingers were in your mouth. I had never heard
any noise come from your mouth before. The littlest things are the
things I enjoy so much. Today I stared at your fingers for such a
long time.*

And a small fulfillment leads to the desire for something more.

Please God—I want to hold Simon without his respirator.

*   *   *

Nothing that ever happens affects only one person. We are connected to each other and to a center like gossamer strands of a web.
A disturbance in one place sends vibrations everywhere. No child
can be dangerously sick alone. The ripples reach all the way up to
heaven. On the way, those ripples pass through brothers and sisters.

Sammy was two when Simon was born. He was the center of the
universe, as are all two year olds. That would have changed with
the birth of any second child, but it changed profoundly and immediately when that second child was one born at twenty-two weeks.

Sammy usually accompanied Tracey to the hospital. At first he
was not allowed in the NICU and so had to be dropped off at the
hospital playroom. She worried about never being able to be with
both her children at the same time but took comfort that Sammy
liked the playroom so much, with its outdoor basketball hoops on
the roof.

Tracey wisely involved Sammy as much as possible in Simon's
life, even though he couldn't see his brother. She devoted a page of
the journal to Sammy at the end of the first week, and he filled it
with scribbles. Tracey labeled the page *To Simon, love Sammy.*
Every time she picked up Sammy from the playroom, she told him
some message Simon had sent to Sammy: " *'You know what Simon
said? He said, "I love my big brother Sammy!"'* Sammy loves to
hear that so much. He gets a big smile. "

Yes, Sammy got a big smile, but that doesn't mean he wasn't a little worried too. At ten days Sammy saw a video of Simon, his first
look at this brother who was getting so much attention. In her journal Tracey wrote to Simon, *"Sammy definitely thinks you're pretty
cool, although he kept saying, 'Sammy's mommy . . . Sammy's
daddy.'"*

And if sharing Mom and Dad was problematic, sharing his blanket was clearly unimaginable. *"Then we talk about all the games*

you guys will play together: hockey, soccer, basketball. But then Sammy says, 'No share BaBa.'" He makes the same declaration later about his toys.

Not wanting to share your *BaBa* with your brother, however, doesn't mean you don't want to pray for him. Tracey recorded Sammy's prayer for Simon in the first days. *"Simon feel better, Jesus. Amen."*

Within a couple of months, Sammy was as much a prayer warrior as anyone on the prayer chains.

> *Your brother Sammy prays for you so much. He just does it all on his own. I'll catch him talking to himself and ask him what he's doing. He laughs and says "Praying Simon." I'm sure these are the prayers the Lord loves to hear.*

A praying two year old. This is a good thing, but not without a price. Tracey agonized about what all these weeks at the hospital were doing to Sammy. "Sammy had to come to the hospital with me every day and go to the nursery. That was as hard as anything, trying to raise my two year old in a hospital setting. Sammy is another miracle in himself. He never complained once about going to the hospital."

Sammy hears Tracey saying this and replies to no one in particular, "I did once." Tracey acknowledges him and then goes on. "Sammy has this obsessive protection of his brother. Always from the beginning. He never had any animosity, just very protective and prayerful and excited about his brother constantly. And never jealous of any extra attention . . ." Never? And then she adds "that I know of."

But if Sammy seemed content with the situation, Tracey was not. "I was split all the time because I could never be a mom to both my kids at the same time. I was like half-time in the nursery with Sammy when I'd go run and see him, then I'd go back and hold Simon for half an hour, and then run back to Sammy. It was terrible. I hated it. Because I was in a situation I couldn't change."

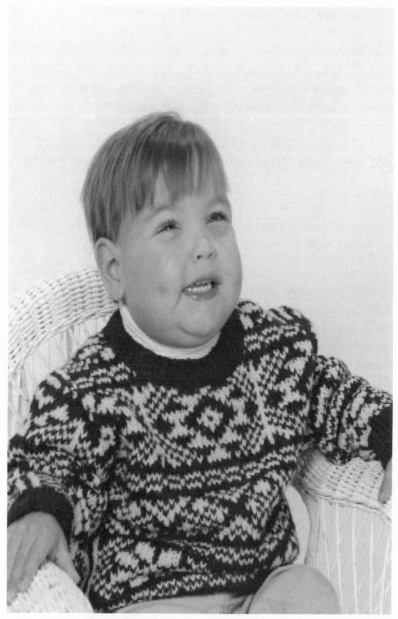

Simon Hagman at three years old

What is a mom to do? Characteristically, Tracey turned it over to God. "I had to trust that God would be the parents to my kids. I had to trust that when I went home at night and Simon was crying in his hospital bed and a nurse was too busy to pick him up that Jesus was going to rock him to sleep. I prayed that all the time. That in the night God would hold him, rock him and be with him. I had to believe that's what he was doing. I don't believe that God said no when I prayed that."

The parental instinct to protect is sometimes overwhelming. Tracey not only stuck Bible verses all over Simon's isolette—like talismans to ward off evil—she put up a sign, *Simon says, "No More Poking Me."* It's a joke of sorts, but not really.

The worst part was when they were trying to get a central IV into your arm. I looked at your face, and it was a silent scream. I just about died. Simon, I can't stand to watch you in pain. I would trade places with you in a second. I wish I were back on bed rest with you safely inside my womb. I feel so guilty that when I was on bed rest I wanted to be off—to deliver you. Oh Simon, I'd do anything for you.

So Tracey was split in two. She gave it up to God as best she could and saw it all as being good for big brother Sammy. "It's been great for Sammy because it's taught him to be less selfish, that he's not the center of the world."

Sammy interrupts again, "Who isn't the center?"

"You."

"What does *center* mean?"

"Like the middle."

"I am the center."

Tracey decides this is something she should explore. "Do you ever feel it was hard when we went to the hospital because Mommy couldn't spend as much time with you?"

Sammy nods.

"Did it make you feel sad?"

Sammy nods again. And adds, "I didn't really like the nursery. It was pretty good but not very great."

"Did you not like it because Mommy wasn't there with you?"

"You were never there with me. You know what? All the other daddies and mommies came in with their little kids, and you don't ever do that with me."

Great. Something else to feel guilty about. Sammy's been a wonderful kid through the whole thing. But he's not above an occasional tug on Mommy's chain.

*   *   *

Eventually the long-dreamed-of, sometimes-feared day does arrive, and you can take your child home. At one time in the whole process you had thought that this would be a kind of ending, a resolution. Now you know it is neither an ending nor a beginning: it is a continuation, but now in a different context.

At one time Tracey grieved, maybe even resented, that the nurses seemed more a mommy to Simon than she did. Now she worried a little that those nurses wouldn't be there all the time. She felt the same about the machines from which she had always wanted Simon freed. And after months of hating to leave Simon behind in the hospital at night, she now wondered if she would ever get a whole night's sleep again.

Simon came home at fourteen months with a hole in his throat. His damaged lungs could not glean enough oxygen from the air. Therefore, he didn't entirely leave behind the machines at the hospital. His tracheostomy was connected by a long plastic line to an oxygen tank.

As the months at home passed, he became more and more active, crawling to the length of his oxygen line, opening cupboards, playing with toys. He discovered he could make sounds by putting his finger in the hole in his throat, causing air to flow through his vocal cords.

This is wonderful progress. But it still isn't *normal*. And normal is what Tracey longed for. Normal means no home nurses, great people though they are, coming into your house for eight to twenty-four hours at a time. Normal means not having a nurse mention that she heard Eric snoring last night. Normal means being able to take your child upstairs without worrying about the oxygen tank.

Normal means taking back your life from medical schedules. After a year at home on the oxygen, Simon was scheduled to have his tracheostomy removed. Three different times the surgery was scheduled, and three times something came up and it was delayed. Each scheduling required a major reorganization of life, and each delay brought exasperation as the possibility of *normal life* recedes again into the future.

Normal also means an end to the miracles.

If you have spent months praying for miracles, why would you want them to end? The answer is simple—because you want them to be no longer necessary. If you are living off of miracles, you are living on the edge.

"I've got all these people praying for this miracle regarding Simon's trachea, and part of me doesn't want another miracle. I just want it to go the way it should go, and it never has."

The way it "should go." That is, the way we want it to go—the way it would go if we were God.

"Part of me says, 'I don't want another miracle. I just want it to be normal.' But, of course, I do want another one." "Part of me" wants this, but "part of me" wants that. Part of me believes this, but part of me sees that. Part of me feels this way, but part of me feels the other. This is human nature, and it is especially the experience of those who love babies born too soon.

Normal also means a break from wrestling with God.

"I'm thinking, *Okay Lord, you've given us enough! I believe you, I trust you, my faith has grown so immensely, and yet I'm just tired of . . .*" Tracey never completes the sentence. Instead she quickly shifts to talking about how faithful God has been. It's as though she is afraid that admitting frustration will anger God and therefore threaten Simon. Tracey admits to feeling a certain pressure to keep her faith up, to perform for God, even though she knows in her head that it isn't necessary.

"I was struggling with the question, 'Does God always heal?' And that's a big question. Because, well, no he doesn't. A lot of people die. But I kept seeing all the Scriptures that said he did. And then I was reading about faith and that you don't receive anything if you don't believe and that you shouldn't be like waves that go back and forth—those who doubt. But then that puts pressure on you and you say to yourself, *If I'm doubting, is my son going to die?*" She resolves it for herself by deciding that God has told Eric and her that Simon will live, but that he doesn't tell everyone the same thing.

But what if—three very human words—but what if Simon *does* die? What if after all the struggle, all the miracles, all the prayers, all the doctoring and mothering, all the tests and procedures and surgeries, all the prayer chains and prayer letters, all the grandparents and friends, all the bargaining with God, all the everything . . . Simon does die?

The broken syntax of Tracey's answer reflects her inner struggle. "If Simon were to die, I would say that I'm at the point in my faith where I believe . . . that I hope . . . until right now I can tell you that my response would be . . . I just . . . God is greater than me."

It is the answer of Job—God made the world, you didn't, so quit trying to figure everything out. And as with Job, "God is greater than me" is not a glib cliché; it is rather the product of reflective suffering. It is a statement of faith, not of bitterness or even resignation. For Tracey, moreover, it is a statement of fact, of how things are. And it is somewhat contrary to her own nature, which is to be in charge.

God's sovereignty does not, however, eliminate human questioning or, in Tracey's case, human honesty. "If God didn't preserve Simon's life, I would have to trust that he just knew better. But obviously, emotionally, it would be extremely hard, and, yes, I would struggle with my faith."

Hard is a word that appears often in Tracey's description of life with Simon. She's too honest to say that it isn't hard, sometimes almost unbearable. But she always insists on the balancing, and greater, truth as reflected in the last words of her journal of Simon's first months of life.

> *Simon, I love you so much. Your life has brought my faith to such heights. I will always remember these months with great joy as well as pain. You are a special, chosen one from God. Never underestimate God's power. He can do anything.*

Great joy and great pain. Both are real. Neither eliminates the other. But joy and faith get the final word. And in Simon's case, the word to date is a very good word.

CHAPTER THREE

B. J.
A SPECIAL CHILD

"I really thought he was a special child."

ALLIETTE PERKINS

*"I could see that they had this unrelenting,
unconditional love for B. J."*

JOYCE, PRIMARY CARE NURSE

Lord, have mercy."

This was Alliette Perkins's simple but profound plea as she drove herself to the hospital. She had been standing in her kitchen doing dishes, just about to go to choir rehearsal. Her husband and older daughters were not at home. Suddenly she felt something like water running down her leg.

Alliette knew what it meant, but she also couldn't believe it. She was only twenty-two weeks along. This couldn't be, but it was. Ready to go out anyway, she decided to drive herself to the hospital. She soon regretted it.

While driving to the hospital she felt that the baby was coming. Clutching the steering wheel, she was afraid the child would be crushed as it was born. The only thing she knew to do was talk to God.

"Lord, have mercy."

And he did. She made it to the local hospital, located next to the largest abortion facility in the state. Go in one set of doors and they will do everything they can to save your baby. Go in the other doors and they will see to it that you come out alone.

Alliette was born and raised in Liberia in western Africa. Bennie, her future husband, came from Liberia to America to study. They became close during a summer trip he made back home in the late 1970s. A military coup led him to send for her to come to America, and they were married in 1980. They had two beautiful teenage daughters, Bennal and Burgette, by the time Alliette became pregnant with B. J.

Bennie wasn't sure another child was for the best. He worried about the age difference between the girls and the new child. He worried about his own age when B. J. would want to play sports with his father.

Alliette recalls, "He was thinking about all those things a father has to do and that maybe he was too old. And we laughed and joked about him maybe not being strong enough to be a father."

Alliette listened to the doubts, but she had none of her own.

"I said, 'No, Bennie. This child is a blessing.' I thought to myself, *This child is special.* I really thought he was a special child because God was so close to me during my pregnancy. There was something different in my life."

If B. J. was special, perhaps it was because he had a special mother. Alliette is a woman who exudes a quiet grace. She is an unusual combination of peace and dignity and generosity. She has a kind of natural nobility that one often finds in Africans.

Alliette is also a woman of relatively few words. There is a mystical dimension to her understanding of life, and such understandings are notoriously difficult to capture in words—explaining, for example, why she felt there was something special about the child in her womb.

"While I was pregnant I would go sit in my car during lunch and

listen to spiritual things. You know, listen to religious programs on
the radio. Every day. And I just felt I was getting closer and closer to
God, not knowing that he was doing this to give me strength, I
think, for what was going to happen in the future."

She also had dreams. One came before she was pregnant.

"I had a dream—a dream about being lifted. I was trying to go up
a ladder, but I couldn't reach where I was trying to go. And three
men were up there, and I reached out my hand because I couldn't
make it, and they pulled me up."

Three men? The Trinity? Something from an African folktale?
She didn't speculate—she just accepted it.

"I felt it was a message. I interpreted my own dream. I just felt
that it was something that God was telling me, that he was saying to
me that whatever situation I got into, I was going to be pulled out of
it."

The situation she got into resulted in her lying in a bed in the
local hospital, talking to a doctor about the prospects for her child's
life. They weren't good. Some decisions had to be made.

Bennie arrived in the middle of the conversation. He made it
clear they wanted to give the child every chance to make it.

"If that's the case, we'll have to transfer your wife. We don't have
the facilities here to save the baby."

"Then that's what we'll do," Bennie replied, "because we want to
give it a chance to live."

Every child should be so lucky.

They were transferred to Abbot-Northwestern. Alliette was fitted
with a fetal heart monitor to keep track of the baby's condition. The
heart beat was strong, so they decided to allow the baby to come in
its own time. B. J.'s own time turned out to be almost twenty-four
hours later—twenty-four hours of labor for a child that could fit in
your hand.

Burgess Jefferson Perkins was born in the twenty-second week of
pregnancy, barely half the accepted time for forming a child. He
weighed seventeen and one-half ounces, and at six and one-half

inches around, his chest was an inch smaller than his head.

He may have been small and have come too soon, but he was a member of the family and the ties were made explicit by his given names. Burgess was the name of his grandfather and his father, though his father uses it only as a first initial. Jefferson was the name of one of Bennie's uncles who had raised Bennie and later been killed in the Liberian civil war.

*   *   *

B. J. did not get off to a good start. At five days a bluish discoloration appeared on his side, usually a sign of a perforated bowel. Because he was not strong enough to endure an operation, they simply put a drain tube into his side to allow the fecal material to come out as best it could.

The second week began worse than the first. He was laboring to live. In addition to the bowel problems, his lungs were not working efficiently, thereby starving the other organs of oxygen.

Things reached the point that one of his doctors thought it was time to stop treatment. He called Alliette at home after B. J. had a particularly bad night. He was swollen and his condition was deteriorating rapidly.

"The doctor said, 'He doesn't look good. I think it's time to let him go.'"

Alliette wasn't sure what he meant.

"He tried to explain that they would just pull the plug, and then they would wrap him up and put him in my arms, until he took his last breath. He said if we wanted a picture with him they could do that. They were preparing us."

But Alliette and Bennie weren't yet prepared.

"My husband said, 'No.'"

Bennie still remembers that moment with pain.

"That doctor said further treatment was a waste of time. He said B. J. would never come home. He gave us the impression we were wasting his time and everybody else's time. But we never thought about stopping treatment."

Alliette went to the hospital for a visit bringing her cousins, two women in their sixties, with her. At this point they met Dr. Hoekstra for the first time. Dr. Hoekstra is no more competent or compassionate than the doctor who thought further treatment unhelpful, but he did have one more idea.

"I think I know what might be wrong, but he would have to have surgery right away. I don't know if there is a surgical team available this morning. I'll check."

Alliette reports him coming back and informing them that a team was available and that the surgery would take place immediately. He then did something that endeared him to her forever and convinced her that God was still keeping an eye on things.

"The thing that touched me most was when he said, 'Let's pray. This is not our doing, it is God's doing. We are just instruments, but God is the one who works through us.' And that's when I said to myself, *This is a Christian doctor.*"

This is not the kind of thing you are taught in medical school, but they were the sweetest words Alliette had heard in a long time.

"So we joined hands and my cousin prayed for B. J. and his surgery, and Dr. Hoekstra said, 'Okay, we're ready to go.'"

It turned out that Dr. Hoekstra was right. The vessel between the aorta and pulmonary artery that naturally closes off in full-term babies was still open. B. J. needed that vessel tied off to have a chance.

"Dr. Hoekstra came back and had a glow in his eye. He said that the surgery had gone well and everything looked much better. So we had hope then. And I felt so close to Dr. Hoekstra from that day on. To tell the truth—I know I shouldn't say this—it was like he was God-sent, and whatever he said after that was the same as from God and was going to be right for me. So I just looked forward to him every day. If Dr. Hoekstra wasn't there, I was going to worry. Even though the other doctors are good doctors, I just wanted to see his face."

*   *   *

Alliette also grew attached to the nurses who took care of B. J., such as Joyce and Shelley. They were two of B. J.'s primary nurses, meaning he was one of two or three children they would care for during their shift. If he was having an especially difficult time, they would care only for him.

Joyce is dark-haired and in her late thirties. She is soft-spoken but strong-willed and an outstanding nurse. Shelley is sandy-haired and in her mid-thirties. Her concern for her patients causes her to question the doctors strenuously about their conditions. She is passionate about the details because she knows details are often the difference between life and death. Both of these women have strong maternal instincts and give themselves completely to their work.

Nurses frequently volunteer to become a primary nurse for a child, sometimes only after getting a sense of the child and of the parents. And sometimes parents request a specific nurse, as Shelley recalls Bennie doing.

"Bennie was recruiting primaries right away. I liked him from the first. He was a really nice guy. Joyce was at the delivery, and he wanted her for B. J."

Joyce recalls being flattered but surprised that Bennie requested her. She thought maybe she had been a little hard on them at the delivery, trying to help them see what might lie ahead.

"I wanted them to be realistic. I was preparing them. I wanted to be completely up front and let them know that things were not going well. You don't want to give false optimism, and I tried to state things as factually as I could. So I was surprised later when I got a call from Bennie at home, and he asked me to be one of B. J.'s primaries. I thought maybe I had been almost cold with them, like 'This baby is going to die, so let's be realistic about it.' So I was surprised and flattered when he called. And I said yes, but I worried about it. Still, I could see that they had this unrelenting, unconditional love for B. J.—they just loved him."

Despite the successful operation on the blood vessel, things kept going wrong for B. J. His bowel continued to be a major problem. By his fourth week he was strong enough for abdominal surgery. What they found wasn't encouraging.

His abdominal cavity was filled with stool. His small intestines had multiple perforations. It was literally broken into pieces. They removed the dead or dying sections of bowel and connected what was left to his abdominal wall, so that future excretions would come out his side.

Two weeks later, things got worse yet. The incision from the abdominal surgery split apart, and B. J.'s intestines spilled out. Nothing can be done when this happens. The tissue cannot hold stitches. Part of the intestines must simply lie outside on the baby's abdomen for the time being.

When things go this bad, some people begin to give up or, depending on one's point of view, get realistic.

Many people pass through the NICU: pediatricians, perinatologists, anesthesiologists, nurses, surgeons, therapists, cleaners, social workers, parents, administrators and so on. Some of them like to share their opinions, informed or otherwise.

A few had opinions about B. J. Some were opinions disguised as a question: "What are you doing this for?"

"This" could refer to any of the treatments B. J. had received, including the decision to allow him to live in the first place. The clear implication was that they were doing too much, that the treatment was too extreme, the odds too low, the best thing being to let the baby die and move on.

But then, these people didn't know that this wasn't just a baby, it was B. J.—Burgess Jefferson, named after his grandfather and uncle, the only son of Bennie and Alliette, the only brother of Bennal and Burgette. And they didn't seem to fully appreciate that this was the only life B. J. was given, and that, for him, there was nothing in this world to "move on" to if treatment was withheld.

The criticism of the treatment, spoken and unspoken, made

things difficult for his nurses, as Shelley remembers.

"It was hard on me as a nurse. I'm trying to do my job, and I get this criticism. I thought, *This is not good, but we don't know.* I'm a strong believer in the idea, 'Have you ever walked a mile in my shoes.'"

We don't know. Yes, there's the rub. Shelley reaches for a photograph sent to her by a proud mother. It shows a former twenty-three weeker, now a healthy-looking six year old heading off for the first day of school.

"We never know at first whether they are going to end up like this or end up dying or with huge problems. We just don't know. But people come by and make judgments without knowing everything, and it makes it hard."

The cards and photographs parents send in about former patients mean a lot to her.

"I don't know if the families know how great it is to get cards and to see how well the children are doing. It's fun to see babies getting better and then later doing well. It makes me feel good about what I am doing."

*   *   *

B. J. was on a respirator from the first, using a tube that ran through his mouth and into the trachea. At two months he pulled out his own tube. They decided to leave it out for a while to see how well he could breath on his own.

Three weeks later it was time for eye surgery. Because of his extreme immaturity, the blood vessels in B. J.'s eyes were devloping abnormally. Laser surgery is used to deal with this abnormal development, but it is a precarious procedure, and blindness may occur despite it. In B. J.'s case, things go half right. The right eye turns out well. In the left eye the retina detaches, and B. J. is blind in that eye.

The experiment of B. J. breathing on his own succeeded for a time but did not last. When he was three months old, five weeks after he pulled out his own breathing tube, a tracheostomy was done. A hole was cut in his throat and a tube was inserted directly into his trachea. This is unusual even for preemies, but it was clear B. J. was going to have long-term breathing difficulties, and this freed him from always having something in his mouth.

*   *   *

When one lists B. J.'s problems this way, it makes his life sound like one unbroken, slow-motion disaster. But that is the problem with only reading the charts. The charts list only procedure after procedure, medication after medication. The charts are full of numbers and jargon. The charts don't tell you about lunch with Mom.

Alliette never quit her job as an accountant at a local college. B. J. came before she would have taken a leave, and after he was born, she decided that it was best if she didn't spend every waking hour thinking only of what was going to become of him.

Alliette had spent lunchtime in her car listening to religious programs while B. J. was developing in her womb. After his birth she still spent her lunches with him.

"B. J. was my lunch. We called the first thing every morning to see how he had done during the night. Then at lunch I would drive over to see him. I had an hour for lunch, and it was twenty minutes each way from work to the hospital. So I would drive twenty minutes there, be with B. J. for ten or fifteen minutes, and then drive twenty minutes back. I didn't eat anything. B. J. was my lunch. Every day."

After work Alliette would come again and stay through the late afternoon and early evening. Then she would go home and make a late dinner for her family.

How much does it really matter to a severely premature child— eyes tightly closed, a tube in its mouth or throat, its brain and other organs not fully developed, often on sedating medication—that its mother is there or not there?

It matters.

Joyce said B. J. knew when Alliette was there, and the machines proved it. One of the many things the machines measure is the amount of oxygen being carried by the blood. It is a key measure of how well a baby is doing, and it is affected by stress.

"Alliette could change his oxygen levels. She was like no one I've ever seen. She would come in and start talking to B. J. and touching him, and you could see the numbers change on the machine. When babies are tense or angry, they often get air hungry. When Alliette was there, we could turn the oxygen down on his respirator."

How does one account for that? To Joyce, the answer is obvious, and she begins to cry as she recalls it.

"Because she's his *mother*."

*   *   *

Alliette made a strong impression on everyone who spent much time with her. The recurring terms used to describe her are an interesting mix of gentleness and strength: kind, peaceful, gracious, strong, thoughtful, determined, focused.

No one can fully explain why Alliette exuded such strength and peace, but Shelley's thoughts are typical.

"She was always at peace, always gentle. It was probably because she was so religious. That gave her peace."

Shelley has her own kind of faith but does not want to cross over appropriate boundaries.

"I want to be accepting of what others need to do to help them cope with their child's hospitalization. I want to be accepting of other people's religious views, even though they may not be the same as mine."

Shelley says she believes in miracles. Her definition of a miracle is more cautious than some, but also apt.

"For me, a miracle is something wonderful happening for the best. I get lots of cards at Christmas from the parents of former patients. Most of them think their child is a miracle. And I believe they are a miracle too!"

One of the things that impressed Shelley was that Alliette's kindness, whatever its source, extended beyond concern for her own family. Shelley remembers her as always interested first in her child, as all parents are, but then also interested in the lives of those taking care of him.

"Her first question was always 'How's B. J.?' But her second question was always 'How are you, and how is your family?' I've never had anyone ask so much about *me*. Bennie was like that too."

"We had a connection. She would say, 'Boys are different. I don't know about boys. You're going to have to teach me.' So I would tell her stories about my kids, and she would laugh. B. J. was her little boy. She had two daughters she loved, and now B. J. was her little boy."

Alliette's little boy needed a miracle—"something wonderful happening for the best." When he was four months old, they did a contrast dye study to see how much usable bowel had developed. The goal since his first bowel surgery at one month was to see if he could grow enough to support continued life. Parts of his bowel were still outside his body, but the crucial small intestine was inside and its present length unknown.

The results were disappointing. An infant needs in the neighborhood of twenty to thirty-five centimeters of bowel to survive. The dye study indicated B. J. had fifteen centimeters, not nearly enough. They would have to operate to confirm what was going on.

At this point Alliette had another dream.

"I dreamed about a child going into surgery, and this man in the dream said for me to put my hand on the child's stomach. And he told me to say a prayer while I laid hands on the child's stomach. So when I woke up I said, 'That's a message for B. J. I'm going to do that before he goes to surgery.' And so that's what I did."

Because of her conviction that God had spoken to her, Alliette felt at peace about the upcoming surgery.

"I knew B. J. was going to be fine. I was relying on that dream from God, because I believe it was B. J. in the dream. It was a message for

B. J. I had trust in God. My faith was strong. My faith in God was the thing that kept me going, because like Dr. Hoekstra said, they are just instruments, but God is the one who performs through them. Even though God does not come down and speak to us, he speaks to our hearts, and we have to believe in what he can do."

Faith, prayers, laying on of hands, dreams. Dye studies, tracheostomies, oxygen levels, laparotomies. The world of the spirit, the world of the flesh. At the point where they meet, the unexpected occurred.

While Alliette and Bennie were in the waiting room during the operation, they got a call from the surgeon. They had found within B. J. some long pieces of small intestine that had not shown up on the contrast study. After they stitched them all together, they had a total of seventy centimeters, more than enough to support life and far more than they expected to find.

It was not more than Alliette had expected.

"When he called, I thought of the dream. I said, 'God planted something there that was not there before.'"

Not there or simply not seen? Take your choice. It's an easy one for Alliette.

"I was having these feelings . . . you know . . . the mother's feelings."

From a physical standpoint this was the first really good news of B. J.'s life. Now there was a chance. He had escaped any major brain damage, and now he had enough bowel to absorb nutrition.

B. J. began to grow.

His nurses took comfort in this unexpected turn of events. Shelley switched shifts so she could take care of B. J. after his surgery. She knew he was still a long way from making it for sure, but at the least it was a vindication that they had not been wrong to try.

"We were all real happy after the bowel surgery. I felt it was sort of an answer to the critics."

Both Shelley and Joyce admit to feeling a special attachment to B. J., something some feel should be discouraged as unprofessional, but which they see as merely being human—and humane. Joyce rejects the idea that one must choose between being compassionate and being competent.

"We need to be compassionate caregivers, not just technically good caregivers. I don't try to bond to a baby or the parents, and I don't try not to. If I do, I do. That's just how I am. Sometimes I just can't *not* bond. I've been criticized for that."

Joyce knows there is a spectrum of attitudes toward the appropriate distance that should be maintained between nurses and patients, and laughingly acknowledges, "I'm on the bonding end." This also carries over into attitudes toward what contributes toward making a baby well and what doesn't.

"Some people don't believe in anything but tangible, medical, factual, touchable things. I don't believe that."

And she's not above spreading a little anonymous propaganda.

"I even put a bumper sticker in the staff lounge that said 'Believe in Angels.' Then I'd hang around and see what people said when they saw it. It stayed up for a while, but it's gone now."

She understands that some people are dismissive of dragging God and miracles and prayers and the like into the NICU.

"Some think people like Hoekstra are dreamers. But for me there are just too many strange things that have happened. It makes you think. There's more to this than nuts and bolts. There's more to this. There is."

*   *   *

Anyone can understand bonding to a perfect baby or to one's own baby no matter what its problems, but what was there about B. J. that would cause a professional medical person to bond to a child who began life with a tube taped in his mouth, obscuring much of his face, another tube coming out of his side discharging feces, and his intestines piled on his abdomen like a mass of giant worms?

Part of the answer, as we have seen, lies in one's feelings about the parents and the perhaps unconscious transferring of those feelings to the child. But B. J. had subtle charms of his own.

Shelley remembers that he had "beautiful, soft, brown skin and brown eyes. He loved to be held."

Both Shelley and Joyce felt he had a distinct personality, something the passing observer would probably not detect. How can one ascribe personality to an infant weighing a pound or two with eyes initially sealed, face covered with tape and often completely silent because of a breathing tube?

The answer is, you simply have to hang around long enough and watch. And watching is Shelley's job.

"These preemies have personalities. There are feisty ones and mellow ones. I get a kick out of the feisty ones. They get a real mad cry when you change their diapers. They show it when they aren't happy, but you can't hear anything because the tube makes them quiet."

Shelley and Joyce identified B. J. as one of the mellow ones. Joyce lamented that he often had to be medicated, which hid his personality, but that he had a kind of presence about himself that was something like the presence people sensed about Alliette.

"He was very sweet and kind of cuddly. He had a very sweet disposition. And I always felt that he was wise beyond his days."

It seems odd to attribute wisdom to someone so small and new and fragile.

"I thought he had this spirit about him. I don't know. It's hard to explain, but he kind of knew what he wanted. I always thought he could see through people . . . see through the ones who weren't really there to support him. I thought he was most responsive to those who were positive about him. Of course, that's maybe what I wanted to see, but that's what I saw."

One thing Joyce is sure of.

"He's his mother's little boy. He was in love with his mother."

Nothing more endears you to a mother than loving her children. There is an old saying, often invoked in politics and war, "The enemy of my enemy is my friend." The NICU version might be "The one who cares for my child is one I care for."

Alliette knew B. J.'s nurses loved him in a special way, as every mother in the NICU must feel, and it made her love them.

"They all care. They all show that they love him so much. They never made me feel they didn't care personally for my baby. They never made me feel they were too tired."

Bennie felt the same way. Despite his irritation with the doctor who he felt gave up on B. J. too soon, Bennie has nothing but praise for his experience with the people in the hospital.

"The whole hospital community made you feel good—everyone from the cleaning crew to the doctors. You knew when you left B. J. at night that he was being cared for."

It is characteristic of Alliette to be concerned that those helping her child might themselves need help.

"I used to say to Shelley, 'Shelley, can't you sit down for a minute?' But they all show so much love and care for B. J. Because they felt he was special. They told me he was special. They got so attached to B. J. They were all very attached to him."

If B. J. was in love with his mother, clearly his mother was also in love with him.

That love showed itself in many ways, not least in her tender taking leave of him every night. She sat with him and often held him from after work in the late afternoon until around eight in the evening, when it was time to go home to care for the rest of her family.

Each night, when the time came to leave, she put him back in the isolette, bent over him, made the sign of the cross on his forehead, and prayed over him the Twenty-Third Psalm:

B. J., the Lord is your shepherd,
You shall not want.
He maketh you to lie down in green pastures
He leadeth you beside the still waters.
He restoreth your soul.
He leadeth you in the paths of righteousness
for his name's sake.

Yea, B. J., though you walk through the valley of the shadow of death,
You will fear no evil.
For his rod and his staff they comfort you.
He preparest a table before you
in the presence of your enemies.
He anoints your head with oil.
Your cup runneth over.
Surely goodness and mercy shall follow you, B. J.,
all the days of your life,
and you will dwell in the house of the Lord forever.

Oh, that each of us had such a blessing on our heads at the end of every day.

*   *   *

Sunday afternoon was the time the whole family visited B. J. together. They would go to church in the morning and then, often with the cousins or a friend in tow, they would go to the hospital. In the first weeks his sisters were hesitant around him. Bennal, fifteen when B. J. was born, worried each time they left him that she might not see him again. Burgette, thirteen, was struck by how frail he seemed.

"At first he looked really small and wrinkly. You could see through his skin almost. I was afraid to touch him. I was scared I was going to do something wrong that would hurt him."

Later on they got to know their little brother better and found out he was tougher than he looked. They changed his diapers and took turns holding him. Burgette liked playing with his big, soft cheeks. Bennal recalls him always smiling and laughing.

This was also the time the family got to know the nurses and the nurses got to know the family. At Christmas, when B. J. was three months old, Alliette gave Shelley and Joyce glass angels.

For six weeks after his second bowel surgery, B. J. thrived. During the seventh, things began to go wrong.

Alliette and Bennie were starting to think about when B. J. might come home when they found that he was not breathing well. B. J. had respiratory problems from the beginning, as preemies often do, but the hope was that he would grow new lung tissue as he got bigger.

A week after the problem became serious, they did an echocardiogram that revealed severe pulmonary hypertension. It was difficult for the blood to flow through the damaged lung tissue. This put a strain on the heart as it worked to pump the blood and also resulted in the blood not picking up enough oxygen in the lungs before it went to the rest of the body.

Simply breathing became hard work for B. J. He was exhausting himself just trying to get air. The doctors decided to paralyze his body with drugs so that he would not struggle. They got permission to use nitric oxide in his lungs, an experimental treatment approved only in severe cases.

The questions returned. How much is too much? Even his primary nurses struggled, as Shelley recalls.

"It was hard because it seemed like he was suffering. He seemed agitated when he was awake, and he was having a hard time breathing. It makes you start questioning how much longer we should continue treating him. I start asking myself, *What happiness is this baby getting from life?* It was all struggle. We were just poking and prodding. That's when I start to feel bad about what I'm doing."

Though lots of people within the hospital have notions about who to treat and how, few really want the responsibility of deciding, not even Shelley.

"I'm glad to say it's not my decision. My job is to do the best I can for the child." After a moment she adds, "I do have opinions though."

And so do others. The critics came out of the woodwork again.

"They would list all the things that were wrong with him, sometimes including his being blind in one eye. That was okay if they were empathetic—'B. J.'s not doing well . . . That's sad'—but it was hard if they weren't. You want the other staff to be supportive."

Things got worse for B. J. His lungs did not respond to the nitric oxide treatment. He went a month under heavy sedation, but it didn't help.

Things also got worse for the nurses. Joyce recalls feeling she had to stand up for B. J.

"I got very defensive when things went bad. People would come by and make some flippant crack about B. J.'s condition, and sometimes I would just snap. I would think, *I don't even want you to come here if you're going to have that attitude. If you feel that way, that's your right, but B. J. doesn't need that kind of presence around him right now.*"

Even though B. J. was totally sedated, Joyce would sometimes rub his back or do something else to comfort him.

"I would get passing comments such as, 'Like he's going to know you're rubbing his back,' and I'd say, 'How do you know? You don't know if he's aware of it or not. Besides, what if it were your baby?'"

What if it were your baby? Yes, there's the catch in all our calculations. How much to treat? How much to spend? Who to try to save? Who to ignore? When to stop trying to save and allow to slip away?

All of these things can be discussed in the abstract. Studies can be made, statistics compiled and analyzed, arguments weighed, charts created, policies invoked. People can form basket loads of opinions, to be asserted respectfully or arrogantly or flippantly or with a broken heart. But what if it is your baby? What if it is B. J.?

Alliette and Bennie decided to continue treatment. They had seen a doctor give up on him before, only to have an operation on the vessel near his heart save his life. Then it had appeared he didn't have enough bowel to live, only to have the bowel operation reveal more than had shown up on the tests. From that point he had seemed to thrive. Now there was another great problem. But hadn't B. J., with the help of God and the doctors, overcome the others? Why would you stop now? What makes this the point past which we will not go?

B. J. answered all the questions himself, as Joyce hoped he would.

"I prayed that B. J. would declare himself. I prayed that he would clearly go one way or the other. We had been very aggressive. No one could say we didn't try everything. Now B. J. needed to declare himself, and, at the end, I think he did."

B. J. began to show signs of kidney failure. He gained a lot of weight because he was retaining fluid that his kidneys should have been expelling. The oxygen levels in his blood began declining.

Alliette remained hopeful but at the same time began preparing herself.

"When he got bad, I couldn't play with him like I used to. And I started to say, 'Lord, if it's your will . . . but give me that peace, give me that strength, because that's what I'll need.' That's what I begged God for."

Her burden began to feel heavier than she could bear. She needed somewhere to lay it down. She laid it, literally, at the cross. B. J.'s decline began accelerating around Easter time. Alliette had been raised a Christian in Africa by her praying grandmother.

"My grandmother and I got up every morning and prayed together on our knees, and then again at night."

The training she received as a child in Africa stood her in good stead a continent away. Alliette knew instinctively where to turn.

"I was at the point where I didn't know where to find that peace and comfort. There was this church right across the street from where we lived. It wasn't our church, but they had these three crosses outside on the grass because it was Easter. And I just went to the cross outside, and I knelt down and I cried. I just prayed and cried."

One can't help but think of another mother who cried for another son at another cross.

"I said, 'Lord, you said we should leave our worries at your feet. And this burden is so heavy. It is hard.' And I was just kneeling there crying, and I said, 'Lord, I'm leaving it at your feet and I'm going. I just can't carry it with me anymore.' And I went."

The end was not long in coming. Everyone knew that now it was just a matter of time. B. J.'s organs began to shut down. The nurses comforted him the best they could.

Shelley thought she noticed a change in Alliette.

"At the end you could tell a difference in her. Before she always had a sparkle in her eye, but now it changed to sadness. She knew he was not doing well, but she was not ready to let go. I think she had to know she had done everything possible for him. One night she wouldn't talk. I asked her, 'Do you want me to leave you alone with B. J.?' and she nodded her head yes."

Near the end, a small incident occurred that demonstrates both something about the effect B. J. had on people and about the character of Alliette. Shelley had to remove some tape that was holding a tube in place on B. J. When the tape came off, it brought part of B. J.'s skin with it, and he began crying. Shelley was mortified that she had given B. J. more pain.

"I went over to the sink and tried to hide from Alliette that I was crying. She came over and hugged me, and I said, 'This is the last thing he needs right now.' And she just quietly said, 'I know you'd never hurt B. J. on purpose.' It just shows how compassionate Alliette is to comfort me when B. J. was so very sick."

Joyce also found herself crying one day near the end. A passing therapist took her to task.

"She said to me, 'You shouldn't be taking care of him. Look, you're crying. This isn't good. What are you doing?' And I looked at her and thought, *You're assuming a lot here. You're assuming that because I'm crying, I can't do my job.* When I think about it now, I think I would be bothered about myself if I *wasn't* crying. When I don't care enough to cry, I think it will be time for me to go. I related with Alliette because I'm a mother too."

Nurses aren't the only ones capable of tears. Alliette remembers the night Dr. Hoekstra came to her with tears in his own eyes.

"He said he didn't think B. J. was making it, and he was crying."

※   ※   ※

The next day some of the nurses came in, even though they

weren't working. They wanted to see B. J. once more while he was still alive.

Early the next morning Bennie remembers them getting a call at home.

"Dr. Hoekstra called and said, 'I think you should all come in.' We knew it was very serious because he had always been very encouraging to us, and if he was saying to come in, well then we knew. . . . And we knew there was nothing else to be done for B. J. If there was something that could have been done, Dr. Hoekstra would have done it."

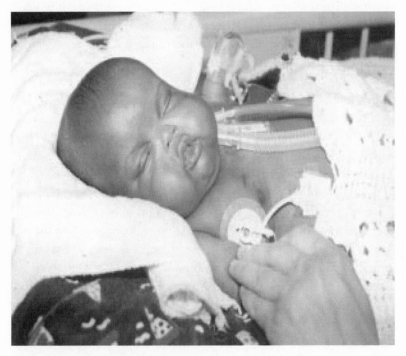

B. J. Perkins shortly before his death

By the time they arrived at the hospital with some of the extended family and friends, the end was only moments away. They took turns holding B. J. But Burgette didn't want to let go of the brother that she and her sister once thought her mother was too old to have.

"I was holding him when he was dying. I was sad, and I didn't want to stop."

Someone said that B. J. should be baptized. There was no chaplain available, and B. J. would not live long enough to have one come in. Bennie remembers them asking Dr. Hoekstra to do it.

"We asked Dr. Hoekstra to baptize B. J. He was kind of apprehensive. He said he wasn't a minister. We said, 'If it's God's will to take him, we want to give B. J. back to God, but we want to baptize him first.'"

Finally Dr. Hoekstra agreed to do it. Someone found a white bowl and put water in it. Everyone stood around B. J.'s crib. Dr. Hoekstra took a cotton ball and dipped it in the water and made the sign of the cross on B. J.'s forehead.

"Burgess Jefferson Perkins, I baptize you in the name of the Father, and of the Son, and of the Holy Ghost."

With those words in his ears, B. J. died.

Free now in many ways, B. J. was freed from the tubes and electrodes that had attached him to machines from the first seconds of his life. Some nurses brought over a blanket they had made for him. They wrapped his body in the blanket, and the family and friends and some of the staff went into a private room with him to take their farewell. Phone calls were made, and Shelley and Joyce drove in to join them.

Everyone sat with B. J. for the next couple of hours. They took turns holding him and talking to him and talking to God. And, of course, they cried.

What do you pray about when the thing for which you have prayed so long, the life of your son and brother, is no longer possible? Bennie knew that prayer is not only about asking, it's also about thanking.

"We thanked God. We thanked him that B. J. had the opportunity to come into this world. We thanked him for the time God had given us to share with him. We thanked God that he had given B. J. life, even though he didn't make it. We thanked him that his will was being done."

And they were wise enough to pray for themselves as well.

"And we asked that his soul be received in heaven. At that point we also prayed for ourselves, that we would live lives that would allow us to see him someday. Because we knew that he would be in heaven."

Alliette did not pray out loud. She sat there quietly with her thoughts. Her thoughts were about others.

"I knew Bennie was hurt. He had grown so close to B. J. They looked so much alike. I was thinking of Dr. Hoekstra and the nurses and all that they had done for B. J."

She was also thinking of the other mothers in the NICU and of their babies. In the time between B. J.'s death and the funeral, she dispersed some of his toys to others with whom she had held vigil over the months for all their babies. She went to Tracey with a little basketball shoe that hung on a string. "B. J. wants for Simon to have his shoe."

While she was thinking of others, they were also thinking of her. Tracey had hoped that Simon and B. J. would grow up to be friends. But it was not to be. For even as Tracey wrote about it in her journal, B. J. was taking his leave. The next day's entry records her painful reflections.

Sweet Simon. We are very sad today. Your friend in the hospital, B. J., died this morning at 8:30. He had been in the hospital for eight months. He was born at twenty-two weeks and has had many complications. His mother and father had such great faith in Jesus. They were such examples to us at the hospital. His mom and I talked about how you and B. J. would play together one day. And you will, but now not until heaven. Simon, my heart aches so much. I feel guilty that you are doing so well, and now B. J. is gone. His mother and I prayed a lot together. She had some beautiful prayers for you. She loved you as much as her little boy. She and her husband amazed me oh so much. Oh Simon, I love you, and I want you to have a full life. One day you will meet B. J. and know what a cool guy he was.

Yes, B. J. was already *a cool guy*. No reason to question it. Nor to ask why one feels guilty when another child dies while yours lives on. It is not rational, but it is very human.

And so is the realization that even as one dies, another takes his place.

It was very sad to be in the NICU without B. J., your friend. There is another baby in his place now, and that's really hard to see. We will go to his funeral Saturday morning.

It should not be so. The world should take more notice whenever any of us leaves it. Something should be different, always, because we are no longer here. But sometimes it doesn't seem so. Yesterday B. J. was fighting, like Simon, for his life. Today someone else is there, and B. J. is gone.

But not before some have paused to remember, and a few never to forget.

This morning we are going to B. J.'s funeral. I really don't want to go, and I feel bad saying that. It's just going to be very painful. I get scared that one day we might have to do that for you. . . . Oh Simon, I love you.

Yes, we want to remember, but not to be reminded. We want to remember B. J.; we do not want to be reminded that the same fate awaits us all—or that Simon is closer to it than any child ought to be.

And so we find in the funeral service the consolation it is designed to give. The ritual is performed, and performing the ritual well eases the pain, especially if that ritual is rooted in the belief that this life is only a prologue to an eternal and happy one.

B. J. now is at peace. His funeral was a real testimony to Jesus. B. J. was a life that was used to glorify our Lord Jesus, just like your life, Simon.

And later,

I went to see B. J.'s mom yesterday. She has such an amazing faith

in Jesus. She has such peace. We do miss B. J. so much. He is such a
sweet boy and now is with Jesus—so much happier.

Wishful thinking? Wise thinking? Neither view can be proved in this life. Certainly it is a response that grows out of believing *more* than is provable, and that seems wise given how little we can prove.

What was the worth of B. J.'s life? Eight months of problems and then death. Never a word spoken, never a deed done. Or so it might seem. It doesn't seem that way to Tracey.

God, you have enabled us to run a fine race with Jesus, just as B. J.'s
mom did. You have encouraged me through her.

And through him.

*　　*　　*

The funeral is a time of grief and goodbye and celebration. Family members fly in from out of town. Members of their church and of the Liberian community are there, as are nurses from the hospital, some of the mothers from the NICU, and Dr. Hoekstra.

B. J.'s family surrounds him in death as they had in life. They sit in a semicircle behind and around his tiny casket. Burgette and Bennal wear light-colored clothes at their mother's direction. Alliette wants a positive spirit at the funeral, not only sadness.

Before the service begins, people come up to see B. J. and to greet the family. B. J. is dressed in a white suit. Alliette has a word with each of them, and there is lots of warmth and hugging. To Shelley, she says, "Thank you for B. J."

In the program is a passage from chapter 18 of the Gospel of Matthew: "Verily I say unto you, Except ye be converted, and become as little children, ye shall not enter into the kingdom of heaven" (verse 3 KJV). The service begins with a song whose words convey the source of consolation that has sustained Alliette and Bennie over the months.

What a friend we have in Jesus,
All our griefs and pains to bear.
What a privilege to carry
Everything to God in prayer.

The singing is loud and enthusiastic. When the pastors from the church speak, the air rings with "amen" and "hallelujah." For some of those from the hospital staff, it is an eye opener. Joyce, for one, had never come across anything like it in Iowa.

"I grew up Catholic in a small German town in Iowa. It was unlike any funeral I had ever been to. There's not a lot of emotion shown at Catholic funerals, at least not in Iowa. But this was very uninhibited. The emotion was intense and very open. I had anticipated that I might be uncomfortable, but I didn't feel that way at all. I found it refreshing. It was so real."

The Scripture reading during the service is also from Matthew, this time chapter nineteen. It recalls Jesus admonishing his disciples for not properly valuing little children: "Then were there brought unto him little children, that he should put *his* hands on them, and pray: and the disciples rebuked them. But Jesus said, Suffer little children, and forbid them not, to come unto me: for such is the kingdom of heaven. And he laid his hands on them" (verses 13-14 KJV).

At Alliette and Bennie's request, Dr. Hoekstra speaks briefly. He says they have gathered to remember and celebrate the life of B. J. Perkins. He points out that the importance of a life is not measured by its length. B. J. had lived only eight months, but the impact of his life on others was as great as or even greater than that of many who had lived to old age. One of the many benefits of B. J.'s life was that it gave many people the opportunity to know and be inspired by his parents. He then directs his comments directly to Alliette and Bennie.

"Today we can only imagine the sense of sorrow and loss which you must feel. However, we are confident that the same faith which sustained you on many occasions during the past eight months will hold you today. In the forty-third chapter of Isaiah, our Lord promises us, 'Fear not, for I have redeemed you; I have summoned you by name; you are mine. . . . When you pass through the rivers, they will not sweep over you. When you walk through the fire you will not be burned; the flames will not set you ablaze. For I am the LORD, your God.' "

They then sing another song. It is the first song that many children learn who grow up in church. It is a very simple song, and it is a heartbreaking song to sing at the funeral of a tiny child.

> Jesus loves me,
> this I know,
> for the Bible
> tells me so.
> Little ones to him belong.
> They are weak
> but he is strong.

Many in the congregation are in tears as the song is sung, including Alliette. "Yes, Jesus loves me." She sits at the head of B. J.'s casket and strokes his head. "Yes, Jesus loves me." From time to time she fusses with his clothes. "Yes, Jesus loves me. The Bible tells me so."

Then it is Alliette's turn to speak. She does not speak long. She thanks God for bringing B. J. into their lives, for blessing them with B. J., even if only for a short time.

Then she asks a question as simple as the song they had just sung: "Who am I going to have lunch with now?"

*   *   *

Bennie does not trust himself to speak. Instead he reads a letter he has written to B. J. In it he thanks each of the doctors and nurses by name, and then tells B. J. what he remembers of their time together.

The service closes with one more song. Everyone stands as they sing "God Be with You Till We Meet Again." They then take B. J.'s casket to the cemetery. He is buried beside his grandfather and namesake. Burgess Benedick Perkins, a man who lived most of his life in Africa, is now joined by Burgess Jefferson Perkins, his grandchild of eight months who was born too soon, placed there by Burgess Benjamin Perkins, a father of two daughters and one son, a man now acquainted with grief, like another man long ago.

*   *   *

The funeral, of course, was not the end. Even now, Alliette feels B. J. is close to her. And to others. Six months after B. J.'s death, one of B. J.'s nurses had a baby. Alliette sent her a note saying, "B. J. is going to bless your baby."

Alliette believes B. J. is praying for each of them. Occasionally Alliette calls up Joyce.

"We are the ones who knew B. J. He lived at Children's. That was his home. We are the people who knew him, and Alliette doesn't want him forgotten. And we don't forget B. J."

Alliette believes B. J. himself wants to make sure he isn't forgotten. On the Easter after he died, near the anniversary of his death, Alliette was getting some things from a closet when B. J.'s Easter basket fell down.

"I just thought that was B. J. saying to me, 'Mom, you forgot to put my Easter basket out along with the girls'!' So I took it and put it out with theirs."

Do those we love stay near us after they die? Many have thought so, though theologians and scientists may frown. Perhaps it would be better to say many have *felt* so, because it is with our feelings that we sense such things, if we sense them at all. Alliette is a quiet, intuitive, peaceful woman—and now a part of her will always be sad. And yet she continues to have dreams.

"I still have B. J.'s picture right beside my bed. And every now and then I dream about a little boy. And sometimes I think it's him. I just feel that he's an angel."

CHAPTER FOUR

BLAKE
NO HOPE BOY

*"You didn't do anything wrong.
It's not going to live. We're sorry."*

ATTENDING PHYSICIAN

*"Rejoice in hope;
be patient in suffering; persevere in prayer."*

ROMANS 12:12 NRSV

Write the stories of a hundred premature babies and you will have a hundred stories as unique as the babies themselves. But within those stories, some things will come up time and again. Surprise, for instance. These babies teach us modesty—modesty about our expertise, about our machines, about our ability to know the future.

Take Blake, for example. He was given up on more times than a skid row bum, and yet he never quit asserting his interest in living.

*   *   *

Marc and Leslie Boudreau were living a garden-variety suburban life. He was thirty-nine and she was thirty-three, and both were working. Leslie is five feet three inches tall with shoulder-length blonde hair and a self-described affinity for talking. Marc is six inches taller and perceptibly quieter, but with a sense of humor that emerges when he is at ease. Both of them like to get all the facts when they are assessing a situation, and with Blake there was a lot of facts to assess.

Marc and Leslie were out of town when things first got interesting. They were in Chicago visiting Marc's father, who was in the hospital with a heart aneurysm.

"I was twenty weeks along at that point—exactly five months. The pregnancy had been normal—no problems at all. I went into the bathroom before we got on the plane to come back, and I was bleeding. I was scared, of course, and so we called the doctor in Minneapolis. They said it was common for women to have bleeding problems and that if it was not real heavy to go ahead and get on the plane and come home."

The confidence of the doctors made them confident as well. Nevertheless, after landing in Minneapolis they decided as a precaution to stop by the hospital on the way home. It was a more momentous decision than they could have possibly known.

"They decided to do an ultrasound. I hadn't had one yet because it was too early. The technician was doing the ultrasound and all of a sudden she just left the room. A different person came back with a gurney. They put me on it and said, 'Don't move.' I found out later that Blake's foot was already through the cervix."

Some kids just can't seem to wait. But like a tulip that sticks its head through the ground too early in spring, they risk a killing frost.

"They said, 'The baby's coming, and there's nothing we can do. It can't survive at twenty weeks, but we can't stop it.' They took us into another room and explained some things to us."

Those things included when life outside the womb was supportable and when it wasn't. They said that sometimes they can sew up the cervix to keep the baby in longer, but in this case the foot was already through the cervix. They would give Leslie a drug to induce labor and take the baby. They were sorry.

Not as sorry as Marc and Leslie.

"They closed the door and we sat there. We decided we had to pray. We prayed and prayed and prayed. We couldn't believe there was nothing they could do, so we just prayed, 'Oh God, if there is something *you* could do . . .'"

Not a very focused prayer. Not perhaps even a prayer of great faith. But it was a cry to God from the heart, and it was all they knew to do at the moment.

Marc and Leslie weren't the only ones praying. They had called a friend from church, Judy, and she and her sister had come to the hospital. It was two in the morning. Judy heard what the doctors had said and then made a pronouncement.

"The baby is going to be fine."

Leslie tried to pass on to Judy the sense of realism that had been passed on to them.

"You don't understand. The foot is through the cervix. It's coming."

But Judy was unfazed.

"I told her the doctors were going to induce labor, and she just repeated, 'The baby is going to be fine.' Then, before she left, she prayed a real specific prayer. 'Lord, push that baby back up somehow. Push that baby back into the womb, Lord. Close her cervix.'"

It was a new way to pray for Leslie.

"We had never prayed that way. We just said, 'Oh Lord, please let it turn out okay. Do whatever you can.' But she's here praying, 'Push the baby back up!' I have to admit, I was thinking she was wacko. She must not have understood what the doctors were saying. There was no way the baby could be saved."

Judy and her sister left. For the next two hours the Boudreaus sat in the hospital room awaiting the inevitable. Around four in the morning, the winds of grace began to blow.

"The door opened again, and we thought they were bringing the drug to induce labor. But instead a completely different doctor walks in the door. And we could see two ambulance drivers out in the hall. She says to us, 'You know, we've been discussing it. If you want to take a chance, we're going to transport you very carefully to Abbot-Northwestern. They'll try to push the baby back up and sew the cervix.'"

"There's nothing we can do." "A completely different doctor." "We've been discussing it." "If you want to take a chance." These phrases are testimony to the seeming arbitrariness of life and death in the modern world—even inside a hospital. Which hospital do you happen to go to? Who's on duty when you arrive? What do they believe about viability? What are their policies? What have they seen before or never seen? Have they just read an article about this or are they still living off what they learned ten years ago? Has an insurance company just given them a bad time about another patient's bills? Do they have a strong value system? Do their personal values matter? Are they tired? Is their shift about to end? What mood are they in? What if someone else had been on duty?

Sometimes a baby will live or die depending on factors that have nothing at all to do with medicine. Frequently it's not a question of skill—or of medical ethics—but simply a question of how one assesses the possibilities. In the end it might be as much a matter of imagination as of science. Can we see a way out for this infant? Is there something we are not considering? Is there really nothing we can do?

Or it might be a matter of who is in the prayer chapel. Unknown to Marc and Leslie, Judy and her sister had not gone home. For those two hours they had been in the hospital chapel continuing to pray.

Leslie will never think about prayer in the same way.

"When the doctor came in and said, 'We are going to try to save your baby,' I thought of Judy and said to myself, *Why ever doubt the power of prayer through this woman!*"

✳   ✳   ✳

Leslie was transported to Abbott-Northwestern. They were able to push Blake's foot back up and sew the cervix closed. This whole episode, however, is akin to stopping the leak in a sinking boat. You are glad the boat is no longer leaking, but you are still adrift in the ocean, and there are fins in the water.

One of the big threats now was infection. The membranes housing the child were not broken, but they were exposed, and there was the risk of infection. They were told they would know within seven to ten days.

An even more critical problem was simply time. The child needed to be kept in the womb for weeks, not days, if he was to have a decent chance. They had been told that twenty-four weeks was the minimum. That meant they needed a month.

Leslie was put in one of the long-term rooms. It had its own small refrigerator and microwave. Her job now was clear—do nothing. Literally nothing. Movement was the enemy.

"I never moved for ten days."

They decided I could try going home. They inserted a pump in my leg that had a drug in it to suppress contractions.

"It was the same drug I was getting through an IV drip in the long-care room. They said, 'Every time you feel yourself having contractions during the next four months, give yourself a dose.' It was supposed to stop the contractions. They put it in my leg a couple of days before I was to go home to make sure it would work. Well, it didn't work. On the second night I started having contractions. Marc had just gone home. I kept pushing the pump, and the contractions didn't stop. I called the nurse in and said, 'I'm giving myself double dosages and nothing's working. It's not stopping them.'"

The nurse checked the monitors and decided to call a doctor. The doctor ordered an amniocentesis.

"They withdrew fluid from the uterus. They told me it should come out clear. Well, it came out dark green. I was infected, and the baby was infected." They called another doctor in.

"They said, 'You're full of infection. He's not going to make it. It's too early. He's nonviable. We're sorry. You did everything you could.'"

They knew mothers tend to blame themselves when things don't work out in the long-term care rooms.

"I had just gotten bathroom privileges, and I was wondering if maybe I had moved too much or something, but they said, 'You didn't do anything wrong. The risk of infection has always been there because the membranes were exposed. It's not going to live. We're really sorry.'"

Up to this point all the focus had been on stopping contractions and keeping the baby in the womb. Now it was imperative to get the baby out.

"They gave me a drug to induce labor, the exact opposite of what they had been trying to do. I said to the doctor, 'Is there any way this baby can survive? Can't we do a C-section or something?' And she said, 'We would do that if we thought it was going to live. But with your infection there's a greater risk to you if we do that.' Different doctors told us the same thing probably four times. They were preparing us for the worst. They all said he's not going to live and how sorry they were. They were really nice about it."

The doctors wanted Leslie and Marc prepared for the worst, but they made preparations in the unlikely case that the inevitable wasn't quite as inevitable as it appeared.

"They said, 'Just in case your baby is okay when it comes out, we will have a neonatology team there.'"

Then one doctor turned to Marc and quietly asked him what has become a standard question in modern medicine.

"He asked real quietly, 'How extreme do you want us to be in saving your baby?' And I said, 'I don't know what you mean. Do what you can to save him. If something stops, restart it.'"

It is a mind-boggling question, "How extreme do you want us to be in saving your baby?" But it is not a foolish or unethical question. The more dramatic the interventions in the beginning, such as restarting a stopped heart, the greater the risk of serious long-term complications. Not all the decisions at this stage of life are medical, and parents carry the largest burden of decision, whether they are prepared for the task or not.

The burden of making life and death decisions is often compounded by near total ignorance regarding the facts of prematurity. Neither Leslie nor Marc knew the basics at that time, as she recalls.

"We didn't have a clue. It was our first baby, and we were learning all this as we were going—very quickly. They would tell us something, and I would say, 'What do you mean his lungs aren't developed?' And they would explain and say we'll have to put him on this machine and this and that. So we just said, 'Do whatever you can.'"

At the point they induced labor, the breathing machines seemed irrelevant. With the overwhelming infection and the lack of adequate time for development, the baby seemed doomed. On the way to the delivery room, the nurses asked if they would like their pastor, who was in the hallway, to be there. Their expectations were clear, and something in Leslie rebelled a bit.

"The nurse said, 'Do you want your pastor to come in the room to baptize the baby before he dies?' I said, 'No,' and I was thinking, *The child is sinless—he will go to heaven anyway.*"

Leslie was not, however, upset at the question. She knew they were trying to help them think through some things they might forget under the anguish of the immediate crisis.

"I never got mad at anything they asked us, because they were just trying to cover all the bases. If a baby does die, and nobody has said anything, well . . . I thought they handled it very well."

But Leslie was also puzzled at what seemed to be mixed signals they were getting.

"At one moment she is asking about baptizing the baby before he dies, and then in the next breath she is warning me that the room is going to be very warm, over ninety degrees, because they want the room temperature as close as possible to the baby's temperature when it comes out. And I'm thinking to myself, *If the baby's not going to live, why does it matter what the room temperature is?*"

Throughout this time there are two distinct currents running through Leslie and Marc. One is the impulse to realism, to the facts as stated, to the great likelihood of death. The other is an instinct for life that says until there is actual death, there is still life, and we must encourage that life in every way possible.

"The whole time we were praying, 'Please, a miracle,' I thought, *There has to be a miracle here.* And there was. I think there were a lot of little steps to a miracle."

Marc didn't know if he should watch.

"I was holding Leslie's hand, and the nurse was on the other side. I didn't know whether to watch or not because I didn't know what to expect. I wasn't really afraid. I just thought, whatever happens, that's the way it's meant to be. So, I didn't even see the baby being born or the umbilical cord cut. The nurses took it right over to the incubator and suctioned his mouth."

Nobody actually said if the baby was alive or not. The nurses then turned and asked Marc a question.

"They asked me, 'Would you like to touch your baby?' And I didn't know if they were asking me this because it would be my last chance ever to touch my baby or what. So I went over to the incubator, and I could see him moving his arms and legs. So I put my little finger in his hand . . . He was alive!"

The delivery doctor then said a strange thing to Leslie, or at least it came out strange.

"She came over to me and said, 'I'm sorry. We were wrong. I think he's going to live.'"

She was not sorry, of course, that Blake had survived, only that they had spoken so pessimistically about his chances.

Blake, the nonviable child, the no hope boy, had made it—so far.

Making it through delivery is a good thing, but it is only the first thing. If you are a twenty-two weeker, surviving the first day only gives you the opportunity to try to survive the second, and then the first week and month and so on. What awaits you are the distinct possibilities of brain bleeds, perforated bowel and failing lungs.

In Blake's case the initial threats are infection and blindness.

"He was nineteen ounces, very good for a twenty-two week baby. But his skin was so thin, they were worried about it breaking open and getting infected, which could kill him. I don't remember exactly, but it's something like you are normally born with eighteen layers of skin and Blake only had three. So they put this mesh on him that they use for burn victims. It was all up and down his body."

Once they were past delivery, Marc gave up on worrying. Whether from faith, fatalism or a certain lack of imagination, he always assumed things would be either okay, or, at the worst, manageable. Even the doctors' attempts to inform them of the serious possibilities were lost on him.

"One of the neonatologists came by and named everything that could go wrong—his hearing, his eyes, his lungs, his skin—all these things. And I was like, 'Aw, whatever.' I didn't really worry about it."

One reason Marc didn't worry was because of his great faith in machines.

"I loved the machines. If it was just some guy giving Blake oxygen with an air bag, well, I don't know. But this machine had graphs and lots of dials on it. I felt better."

Perhaps he believes in machines because his own life depends on them. As a pilot for Northwest Airlines, he bets his life every day that machines will do what they are supposed to do. He transferred that faith to the NICU.

Leslie liked the machines too but not in quite the same way.

"The machines were his life—to me, they were his lifeline."

Interestingly, they finish the same sentence in very different ways. Marc says about the machines, "They look so . . ." Leslie finishes his sentence with the word *intimidating,* but Marc finishes with *complex*. Then he adds, "I'm thinking, *If something is that complex, it's going to help*."

One is tempted to say this is a guy thing. He trusted the machine because the machine was designed to do a job, one he felt incompetent to perform himself. One of the few times Marc was afraid was when Blake was detached briefly from the machine and entrusted to him.

"The first time I got to hold him they took him off the ventilator and handed him to me. All the bells and whistles started going off, and I said, 'Put him back, put him back. I don't want to hurt him. Put him back.'"

Marc also believed in the expertise of the medical people.

"The doctors were so good. Whenever anything came up, they always said, 'We can do this or that.' There was never a time when there was nothing that could be done. There was always a treatment."

Marc and Leslie made a mistake early that many parents of severely premature babies make. They assumed Blake was just a smaller version of a full-term baby. Marc remembers, "I thought he was just small. He's little."

At first Leslie even wondered why the last part of pregnancy was even necessary, because he looked so complete.

"I thought, *What do the other four months in the womb do?* Because he was a perfect little human being. He was fully developed—on the outside. I thought he was perfect but little."

Her naiveté did not last long. "Well, then we found out what the other four months do!"

One thing they do, among many, is allow the eyes to develop. As with others, the possibility arises that the abnormal development of blood vessels in the eye will cause the retina to detach and result in blindness.

Typically, Marc didn't think Blake would end up blind. He adopted his usual view that there was always something that could be done.

"I never thought he would be blind. I thought, *Well, they have this laser surgery,* and we talked to the doctor. I just never really worried about it."

Leslie worried. She worried whether they had what it takes to raise a child with serious disabilities. How do you cope with that? What does it do to your life? What's it like for the child?

They even found themselves mentally negotiating over what disability they would rather Blake have. Leslie recalls that blindness was the one they feared most.

"We both said we'd rather he not be able to walk than not be able to see, because at least we could take him places, let him see the beauty—even if he were in a wheelchair. We were sort of picking things."

It didn't take them long to realize that these things were not in their hands.

"It suddenly occurred to us that we couldn't think this way. No one is given the choice. Besides, even if you have a perfect full-term baby, something can happen later that causes a disability. It's totally out of your hands."

And things got worse. At the same time the doctors were telling them that Blake was at maximum risk for blindness, he was also failing every hearing test. Blind *and* deaf? There are limits to what one can contemplate.

"I kept thinking, 'We can't handle this. At least *I* can't handle this. I can't believe this is being put on us.' "

Leslie then did something very wise—she started collecting stories.

"I started talking to people. I got phone numbers from the hospital and social agency of people whose children were blind because of premature birth. I'd talk to these people—mostly mothers—and I'd hear the child playing in background. They'd be spinning on something and laughing, and I'd get off the phone and think, *Wow! They sound so good.*"

Having a child like Blake introduces you to a community of people with similar experiences that you never knew existed. Leslie found out that a woman at the large company where she worked had a seven-year-old boy who was blind for the exact reasons that threatened Blake.

"She came to Children's while we there, and she had her son with her. He had detached retinas because of his prematurity. One day the doctors had told them that their son's blood vessels were bulging, and the next day they were told the vessels had burst overnight, and their baby was blind."

This is not normally the kind of story you would want to hear while your own child is facing the possibility of a lifetime of darkness. But blindness was not the main point of the young boy's life.

"He was an amazing little boy. For instance, he began quoting Bible verses while we were standing there in the hall—this little blind kid. He can't see, but his hearing and memory and everything just pick up. He sat there quoting long passages of Bible verses. People were stopping and listening to him, including the janitor. It was very encouraging."

Leslie is further encouraged when the mother tells her about the school districts, the buses that pick blind kids up and other practical details. It becomes clear that blind kids have a life, a daily life of going and doing and accomplishing. Leslie begins to visualize the possibility of putting together the seemingly contradictory concepts of disability and normalcy.

Their pastor reinforces the message on a more theological level.

"Our pastor just kept saying over and over again, 'God put Blake on this earth for a purpose. If he's blind, if he's deaf, if he can't walk and talk—he's here and he's going to have a purpose in your life—in everybody's lives.'"

Leslie and Marc finally experienced a peace about Blake's potential problems, though for different reasons. Marc was at peace because he didn't think it was going to happen, and if it did, "then there are people out there who can help us, and we can read up on it." Leslie was at peace because, though she expected Blake *would* be blind, "I now felt we could handle it." She felt they could raise a blind child because she had talked to others who were doing so successfully.

*   *   *

It seems it should be enough that one has to deal with life-and-death issues surrounding the newly born, but Marc and Leslie found some of the same issues facing them from the other end of life.

Marc's father, whom they were visiting in Chicago when Blake's adventure began, was in the hospital with an aortic aneurysm and other problems. After a series of setbacks, his condition had declined. He was struggling for life at the same time as his grandson, and neither was being given good odds.

The doctors asked Marc's mother if she wanted her husband hooked up to a life-support machine. At first she was against it, but Marc's confidence in machines carried the day.

"I said to her, 'Well, personally I would try something. If my heart stopped in that situation, I would want somebody to give it a shot. Give it a couple of tries. Then if it doesn't work, and the doctors say there's no point in continuing, well, that's fine. It's like when the doctor asked me how far we wanted to go in saving Blake, and I said, 'Do what you can.'"

The Boudreaus can't think about Marc's father's situation without thinking about Blake's. In each case they were faced with the question of whether to resuscitate if prospects looked dim. When life is slipping away, how loudly do you call to bring it back? When are we wise to let it go, perhaps with tears and gratitude, and when are we obliged to do everything possible and more to keep it with us? If there are those who cling too tightly to another's life, there are also those who shoo it away with too little regard.

Leslie is astonished that some are so arbitrary about life and death.

"In some states they won't even save children at certain gestational ages because it costs so much money. They're going to have so many problems, and the state is going to have to pay for it. They explain ahead of time that if your baby is born before twenty-four weeks, it's too bad, there's nothing they can do."

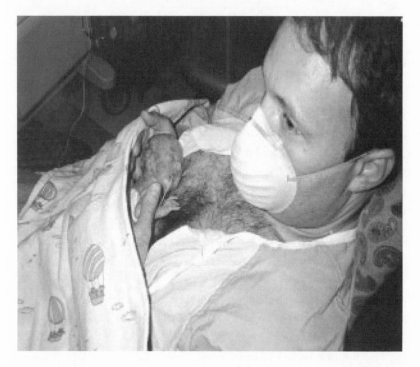

Marc doing kangaroo care (skin-to-skin contact) with one-month-old Blake

She has a hard time believing that some parents wouldn't even try to save a baby.

"In other situations they tell the parents, 'Look, your baby is not yet twenty-four weeks—how far do you want us to go? Because if we keep resuscitating, he will have lots of problems, and it's going to cost x amount of money.' And then the parents have the option of saying, 'Don't even try.' That floored me at first. I thought, *Why wouldn't you at least try?*"

Why does Leslie say "at first"? Perhaps because she knows more now about how difficult those decisions are and how tangible are the possible disastrous outcomes. She pulls back a bit.

"But then on the flip side, I'm not them. I don't know what's going through their minds. There *is* a lot of money involved. And what kind of life do some of these children live when they can't see, they can't hear, they can't move, and they don't know anything of the outside world? Oh, that's hard."

Yes, it is hard. Anyone on either side of the issue who thinks it isn't lives too much in the world of theories and abstractions. But Leslie, given what she now knows, thinks they would have to come down on the side of giving every chance to life.

"I would hate to make that decision. But in our situation, if he hadn't come around the first time, we would have said try again. We talked about it. If it still didn't work, would we say yes the third time—with the possibility of things just getting worse? Yes, I think we would probably say yes every time."

Marc had the same attitude toward his father, but it wasn't unanimous.

"My mother said, 'Your father wouldn't want to be kept alive.' She told the hospital not to try to resuscitate him if something happened. I was there at my parents' house with my brother, and we were giving her ideas, but she made the decision. She went to bed, and my brother and I kept talking. He more or less agreed with my mom that we shouldn't try to keep dad alive. We talked and talked and talked. Then I said, 'If something happens, I would at least try.' So then I woke up my mom and told her what I thought, and she called the hospital and told them, 'I've changed my mind. If his heart stops, you should try to restart it.'"

Leslie adds, "All it took was your opinion, which she was probably waiting for."

It is unsettling that such things come down to opinion. Things were easier when there was much less we could do. Assign life and death to God or to nature and there's little else to do but tell the dying we love them and perform as best we can the rituals of death and departure. But increase our ability to have a hand in the decision, whether through medicine or machine or social policy, and we introduce the agony of choosing.

In the case of Marc's father, the choices didn't matter. Despite the decision to do what could be done to keep him alive, he died when Blake was ten days old, at the age of sixty-nine. The generations passed each other without quite making contact. Perhaps there was a brief wave and nod in some order of reality we know little of.

It was a difficult time for Marc. He went to the funeral of his father in Chicago, not knowing for certain that his son would still be alive when he returned. He had gotten used to praying for the two of them together. Leslie recalls that they had linked their two fates, perhaps unconsciously, counting on their prayers to be efficacious for both.

"We thought for sure Leon would make it because Blake was doing well. We prayed for that every night. But not every prayer is answered the way you want it to be. We found that out."

They learned that prayer is not like ordering Chinese food off a menu—"We'll have an order of this and two orders of that." It's closer to faithfully planting a crop, tending it as best you can, then waiting to see exactly what kind of harvest you will eventually reap, if you reap at all.

"We had also prayed, when I was first hospitalized, that our baby would go to full term. That didn't happen. So for a while we thought, *What's going on? We did everything right. Why did this happen to us?* Which is horrible and selfish to say—'Why us?'—when there are a million bad things that happen to people every day. And ours wasn't as bad as many others, but to us it was huge."

Leslie's faith has taught her to look for silver linings even in what seem like disappointments.

"Okay, God didn't answer that prayer the way we wanted. We didn't go to nine months. But look at all the people we came in contact with. All the people at the hospital and all the people at church and at work, and all the people we share Blake's story with, including the ones Marc corresponded with on the Internet. We wouldn't have any of this if Blake had been a normal, full-term baby. Our lives would be a lot less now."

Among the people they came in contact with was a couple who lost premature triplets shortly after birth. The parents each held one child and the doctor held the third as the infants passed away. That family later discovered they could have no more children. How did they react to tragedy? They dedicated themselves to raising money for the hospital to buy respirators, so that other children could have a better chance at life.

Another couple they met was in the hospital with their second premature baby. The first child had died two hours after birth. He had been born when no one thought anything could or should be done to try to save a baby that premature. He breathed on his own for two hours while she held him, and then he died.

And now a second son had been born, this time at twenty-four weeks, and even though he could not breathe on his own, they resuscitated him three different times. The mother felt she had learned something from the decision not to treat her first child, and so she asks them to try everything for this one. Leslie says to the woman, "I think your first baby was a sacrifice for this brother," and the woman responds, "Yes, that's exactly how I see it."

And though he did make it, this second son had serious bleeding in the brain, became blind in one eye and has multiple long-term problems. And Leslie couldn't help but feel guilty that Blake was doing so well while this other woman's child was having major disabilities.

"They were about two weeks behind us. At each stage, with the eyes and the brain scans and everything, they would ask how Blake had done, and we would say 'perfect.' Then they would get their results, and it wouldn't be good. And when that happened, or a baby would die, I would think, *Did they do something wrong?* But then I look at all the things we've done wrong in our lives and realize the same thing could have happened to us. I don't think your sins are taken out on the baby.

But you wonder why it's so different for one over another. You do."

Perfect—that's the word Leslie uses to describe how things turned out for Blake. It's not much of an exaggeration. His retinas did not detach. Though he wears glasses as a toddler, he is not going to need all those services for the blind that Leslie uncovered. All his brain scans came back normal—no bleeding, decreasing his risk of cerebral palsy. He finally passed the hearing tests, as preemies often do after a series of failures. His lungs developed well. He had no problem with his intestines.

Blake, in fact, is a poster child for what is possible with a baby born at twenty-two weeks of pregnancy. He is a counterargument to any official policy that says these kinds of babies should not be treated, just as other cases can be used to defend such a policy.

Perhaps Blake is an argument against any inflexible policy of any kind. He is a testimony to the fact that we really do not know how any of these children is going to turn out. In this, as in so many areas of life, there are no guarantees and very little certainty. There is only hope and skill and prayer and mutual support.

Hope is, in fact, the word Blake's pediatrician uses when speaking of him, as Leslie recalls. "He said to us, 'I tell other people who have premature babies about Blake. Blake is my hope story. I tell your story to so many people to show them that there's hope.'"

It is not only other parents who are encouraged by Blake's story.

"We got an incredible letter from one of Blake's nurses. She said she had been a primary nurse for another baby who had died. The baby's parents blamed her, and she felt so bad that she decided she would never again get close to parents. She said, 'And then you two—you three—came along and restored my faith. I really needed you to be here. Blake was my boost.'"

And of course Leslie and Marc are themselves different because of this experience. It's changed how they see the world. Marc says, "I'm more aware of life in general."

Leslie is more specific.

"It has changed our prayer life and our closeness to God. And I'm more sympathetic to people who don't have perfect children or what people think of as perfect children. I used to think those parents must feel they have this burden to bear. I don't think that way anymore. I think they just accept that this is their child and they go on with life."

Blake Boudreau enjoying his second birthday

The Boudreaus have also learned that you don't have to go through something like this alone. In fact, you almost can't, even if you wanted to. Too many people have been through it themselves, and too many people care. Say the words "premature baby" in any room of six or more and you will find someone who has a story.

When she investigated the resources available for disabled children, Leslie discovered an entire parallel universe of people and institutions that were available to lend a hand.

"I couldn't believe it. I would never have known that so much was available. I tell people about it. It's incredible the number of people that will help."

The word *hope* comes up again.

"We learned never to give up hope. No matter how bad it seems, there's always hope . . . in any situation . . . even if it doesn't turn out perfect."

Marc adds a qualifier.

"Hope or help. There's always hope or help."

And usually both.

Even before Blake was out of the woods, Marc and Leslie decided to start trying to have a second child. If Blake died, the child would help fill a void. If Blake made it, the child would be a companion, whether Blake was perfect or not.

They became pregnant and this time went for an early ultrasound in case they would need again to sew up the cervix. They brought Blake along. Leslie told the technician that she was here for an ultrasound. The woman looked at her and then over at Blake in Marc's arms.

She asked, "Is that your baby over there?" and Leslie said yes. "You don't remember me, but I'm the one who did the ultrasound. I'm the one who found the foot in the cervix."

Leslie smiled. "You're the one who left the room and never came back."

The technician responded, "I didn't think there was any hope."

After having this new ultrasound Leslie went into the bathroom. When she came out the woman called her over.

"Leslie, I want to show you something. I just dug this out of the file."

She put an x-ray up on the screen.

"There's a picture of Blake with his foot sticking out of your cervix."

"You never showed me that."

"I know. I couldn't. I didn't think there was any hope."

CHAPTER FIVE

ANNA & LIAM
AT THE CENTER
OF THE CIRCLE

"It was such an amazing thing.
It was this full circle, with this
beautiful love that still came
out of her and never ended."

TINA RAHR

Things are being prepared for our good long before our birth. Our stories do not begin and end with us. They are part of larger stories into which we are born, and our stories give birth in turn to other stories.

Anna and Liam were born, after great trauma, to Tina and Laurie. The significance of their births, however, cannot be fully understood without knowing something of the story of Tina's unusual and somewhat mysterious grandmother. Events in the grandmother's life began a circle long before Tina was born that would be completed with the birth of Tina's children long after the grandmother had died. Such is the nature of things in a universe that is ruled by forces far beyond the comprehension of physics.

*   *   *

In the late 1940s Susan Tucker Malarkey left her wild, philandering Irish husband. She was not a religious woman, but over the next five years she began to develop an interest in spiritual things. She met an Episcopal nun who had founded a convent in New York City, The Community of the Holy Spirit, and they became friends.

Eventually Susan Tucker Malarkey had a calling—a literal calling. She heard a voice call her into service, and she heeded the call. She joined Mother Ruth's community and spent the rest of her life there, a great deal of it in prayer. And, in time, one of the central objects of her prayer was her granddaughter Tina.

*   *   *

Tina loved her grandmother, but she didn't think much about prayer until life presented her a challenge that left her little to do except pray. That challenge was in the form of Anna and Liam, though at first they had no names.

Tina Rahr and her husband, Laurie Lane-Zucker, had difficulty getting pregnant. They consulted the best fertility specialists in New York City. Tina refers to the whole prolonged experience as "an odyssey."

They found that fertility doctors are sometimes more interested in numbers than they are in people. Their doctor was very successful at what he did, yet somewhat cavalier about the significance of each life he helped create.

Tina and Laurie are not among those who applaud sextuplets and the like as an outcome of fertilization treatment. Laurie, editorial managing director of a national environmental organization, thinks such multiple births are irresponsible. So when an early ultrasound indicated that two eggs had been fertilized, they were not happy, as Tina recalls.

"We were really upset, because I only wanted one. I must have

been deluding myself in thinking I would have only one after all these
fertility drugs, but I was upset, and I called the doctor. And he just
callously said, 'Oh, you can just have a reduction.' It was just the way
he said it. He didn't say, 'We'll sit down and talk about this.' He just
flippantly said, 'Oh, you just reduce.' I found it really callous."

We encourage life. We reduce life. And we market our ability to
do both. If it didn't bother the doctors, it bothered Tina and Laurie,
even though it had been their decision to enter into this "odyssey."

Tina remembers that it was much more than taking some pills
and then waiting to find you were pregnant.

"They pumped me up with drugs, including a very aggressive one
that had just been approved by the FDA. It made my ovaries go crazy.
They swelled up like grapefruit. I gained twenty pounds in fluid and
was very sick for two weeks. The ultrasound showed a lot of follicles
that could end up being fertilized, and I told them I didn't think I
wanted to go through with this, but they said not to worry.

"I went home and thought about it some more and called and
said, 'Maybe we should skip this cycle.' The nurse said she would
talk to the doctor. She called back and said, 'No, let's go through
with it.'"

Today Tina is amazed that she allowed others, because they were
supposedly experts, to have such influence over what should have
been Laurie's and her decision.

"I just didn't know about the stories. Since then I've heard all
these stories. I learned the hard way. I didn't have any friends that
were going through this. I wasn't strong enough to know that my
intuition was right."

Women tell other women their stories and not only pass on wisdom but also the strength to direct their own lives.

Laurie is more philosophical. They knew they were entering a
process that was not wholly natural. Nature would have left them
childless. For better or worse, they were putting themselves in the
hands of people who knew more about these things than they did.

"It is a process, and it's thoroughly humanly manipulated. At a certain point you have to trust the doctor."

But that was exactly what Tina never did.

"I never trusted that doctor. Even before he checked me out, there was something about him even at the personal level that offended me. Things he would say. He was young and aggressive, and sometimes we couldn't believe the way he would talk to us."

There may have been reasons he was that way. After all, he had competition.

"I think a lot of these doctors want good statistics, and they'll do whatever they can to get these women pregnant. Their success rate as doctors is based on how many women get pregnant, not on how many women deliver healthy babies. It's very deceiving. They're comparing their percentages with other doctors, and that puts pressure on them that is not necessarily in the best interest of the parents."

Tina and Laurie are not ungrateful that modern medicine made it possible for them to have children; they simply believe that a very stressful and uncomfortable time could have been better if they had been treated more humanely, and less like another notch on a fertility doctor's gun.

If getting pregnant was bad, being pregnant was worse. Tina began by being sick.

"It was not pleasant. The first trimester was hell. I was very sick and vomiting all the time. At fourteen weeks I was just starting to feel good, like a normal pregnancy. I was starting to feel myself again. We were in Montana at a ranch my parents have. I dove into the pond and felt something pull in my uterus. I don't know if the diving caused it, but about four hours later I started bleeding—not heavily but very bright red blood.

Tina thought she was miscarrying. The next day she went into a local hospital. The doctor did an ultrasound and said he thought he detected a little tear in the placenta. He told her to take it easy for a week and that it would probably heal itself. The bleeding stopped. But a couple of weeks later, after they were back home in Massachusetts, she started waking up in the middle of the night with severe cramps.

Tina's local obstetrician could find nothing wrong and recommended against bed rest when she asked about it. "He said it wasn't proven to be beneficial and added, 'You'll go crazy in bed.'" He proved to be prophetic.

The cramps persisted and at twenty-one weeks Tina decided to try again to get some answers. She went to "the man who wrote the book on ultrasounds" but got no further insight.

The next week she flew to Minnesota for a weekend to visit her parents and childhood friends. Her local doctor told her she didn't want to be on a plane if labor started, but she joked that they had good hospitals in Minnesota and went anyway. What he didn't know, but might have discovered if he had checked her at the time, was that she was in labor already.

Her friends in Minnesota were giving her a baby shower not long after she arrived, and the cramps began coming every five to ten minutes. Tina describes the cramps as "riveting," an apt metaphor on many levels.

"I was asking all my girlfriends who had all had babies what was going on, and they just stood there. I was going 'uunnh' with every cramp and wondering, *What's wrong with me?*"

What was wrong was that she was in hard labor. Her mother called her own doctor, who saw Tina immediately. The contractions were now three minutes apart. He found that she was 100 percent effaced and that the head of one of the babies was pushing against the cervix, ready to be born.

The birth of twins at twenty-two weeks would likely have been a disaster. The fertility doctor would have his desired statistic, but Tina and Laurie would likely have only had two children to mourn and bury.

Tina was immediately put on a drug to stop labor. It worked. She was stabilized. She was also stuck. She had gone to Minnesota for the weekend; she stayed six months. It looked like an unlucky break. It may instead have been the best thing that ever happened to her. It may have been a delayed answer to a grandmother's prayers.

First it was the fertility game, now it became the waiting game. Tina was given a long-stay room in the hospital, and the whole point of her life became for nothing to happen. Nothing. No cramps, no labor and, for heaven's sake, no delivery. Initially the goal was thirty weeks. At thirty weeks everything is in place and functioning. Survival rates with good outcomes are very high. Even twenty-eight weeks would be acceptable.

"They made a big deal out of it. We were marking off each day on the calendar. They said, 'Every day we can keep them in is three days they will not have to be in the NICU.'"

Tina's mom's doctor was encouraging. Some of his partners were less so. One partner came in shortly after she was admitted and was very blunt. "I really don't think that you'll be able to carry these for more than another few days." And he made it very clear that birth at twenty-two weeks would be a terrible thing.

These kinds of comments, and bad turns of other kinds, were more than enough to send Tina into long spirals of despair. Up to this point she had, by her own description, lived a rather charmed and somewhat sheltered life. She had grown up in a prosperous home, been sent early to the right schools, had all the experiences in life that prosperity and good breeding can afford. She was, and is, a beautiful young woman, and she could always choose from a crowd of handsome admirers. She had been on her own in her twenties, living in New York, pursuing her interest in photography. She had married a good man who shared her values, and their jobs allowed them to work together on the same magazine. Life seemed good. It did not prepare her for this.

✻   ✻   ✻

Tina might not have made it without the nurses. Laurie had to go back to Massachusetts to work. Tina's mother was extraordinarily helpful throughout, but she could not be at the hospital all the time and particularly could not be there in the middle of the night when some of the worst moments came.

"The nurses on that floor were so wonderful—Elaine and Annie-Cecile and Debbie. They were just incredible nurses. And Sandy and Jeanette saved my life. They made it possible for me to survive those months. I tell you, nurses like that should be given much more credit than they get. They were so supportive, day in and day out. They would say, 'Tina, you can do it.' They were so optimistic. They'd say, 'I believe in this. You can do it. You can hold on. These kids can stay in there. It's going to be okay.' Elaine would say, 'Trust in God. It's going to be all right.' "

Tina cannot talk about Elaine without starting to cry. "Elaine was the most amazing nurse. She had been on that floor forever, maybe twenty years. Her husband was dying of lung cancer, and yet she'd come in just to help me get through."

*   *   *

Tina had never experienced a long hospital stay, or watched up close as life hung in the balance. Laurie, on the other hand, knew all about it. In fact, his childhood had been largely defined by such things.

His father was past fifty when Laurie was born. He had a major stroke two years later and was in a coma for months. When he came out of the coma, his personality had changed.

"Over the course of the next twelve years he had numerous other strokes. So a central part of my childhood was spent going to nursing homes, halfway houses or hospitals, depending on what state of impairment he was at. He would have a stroke and be paralyzed and then slowly get back some function and then have another stroke. So as a child I was in a rather unique position, particularly in regard to my friends, of having a sick father who I often had to treat as someone I was taking care of."

Laurie's experience as a child shaped his response to the medical crises of their pregnancy.

"I'd been through a long-term illness with someone close to me, and the attitude I came out with was, 'That's just the way it is.' I never asked, 'Why me?' or 'Why us?' So when Tina was in the hospital and the kids were born, it felt similar to when my dad was ill. We've been given this thing to deal with, and we're going to deal with it."

Tina and Laurie's way of "dealing with it" was different in significant ways from how other couples in this book dealt with their crises. They were not as inclined, for instance, to turn immediately to God for intervention or support.

Again, Laurie's upbringing was a factor.

"I was raised a Theosophist. My father's parents were Jewish, but he decided quite early that he didn't want to practice Judaism, and he adopted Theosophy. My mother was raised in the Church of England, but my father thought it was way too strict. She rejected it and embraced Theosophy too.

"Theosophy is very pluralistic. It assumes there is some truth behind all the world religions. We went to a lodge in New York. There were many elements of Christianity, as well as Buddhism, and I was taught about reincarnation. They would sometimes talk about what I would call 'the Christ force,' but they certainly didn't talk about Christ as much as the Episcopalians or others. The Buddha was a highly respected entity."

Laurie no longer considers himself a Theosophist, but he's not exactly sure what to call himself, or even if he needs to call himself any one thing.

Tina's religious background was more tenuous than Laurie's, even though it was more traditional.

"I was brought up Episcopalian, but we never went to church. I think when my grandmother became a nun it sort of pushed my mother in the opposite direction. It was very difficult for the family to accept my grandmother entering a convent. My mother was about twenty-five and going through a difficult divorce from a Marxist, and maybe she felt abandoned by my grandmother. The convent was very strict in those days, and there was contact with the family only a couple of times a year. I didn't grow up going to church. We weren't atheists or anything. It just wasn't part of our lives."

During her twenties, while living in New York City, Tina attended a Unitarian church. "I loved its flexibility and simplicity, and its embracing tenets from all different kinds of religions." Tina first met Laurie at this time, and they went to the Unitarian church together. Laurie had previously attended an Episcopalian prep school. He found the Episcopalians and Unitarians compatible in many ways with his Theosophist upbringing.

At the same time that Tina was happy in her Unitarianism, however, she was also getting to know her grandmother better.

"While going to the Unitarian church, I was visiting my grandmother at the convent. I grew very close to her. I would attend Sunday vesper services whenever I could. I didn't quite understand it because I had really never gone to church before. It was a struggle to get right into those services, but I knew there was something going on that I was meant to understand and investigate further. Anyway, I grew very close to Grandma, and that community actually became like my family. And they think of me that way, and they are like godparents or grandparents."

Like any good family, the sisters encouraged Tina in her gifts, even when it was a bit inconvenient. The Community of the Holy Spirit makes a point of fostering creativity and the arts. Tina was studying photography in college, and the sisters allowed her to photograph the various aspects of their daily lives, both the mundane and the sacred, though they make no clear distinction between the two. It was also a way for Tina to get closer to her grandmother.

"My grandmother came from New England originally, if that tells you something. She was a reserved, noble woman. You weren't scared of her, but it wasn't like 'cuddling up to grandma' either. There was this dignity that you respected. I decided my way of getting to know and understand my grandmother, and of establishing a relationship with the convent, was to do a photo essay on the nuns."

Tina came over from Sarah Lawrence College as often as she could over three or four months to take photographs. Some of the nuns weren't thrilled about it, but her grandmother knew it was another step in completing the circle.

"The shutter on this Nikon camera was so loud. The first thing I photographed was the vesper services, and some of the nuns thought, *Oh my goodness!* But my grandmother was so good and understanding. She was great."

Susan Malarkey took the name Mary Monica when she joined the convent in the 1950s. At that time the sisters' contacts with the external world were much more limited than they are today, as her former husband discovered. He ended up marrying the woman with whom he was having an affair at the time of the breakup of his marriage to Tina's grandmother. Later he decided he had made a mistake. In a scene worthy of the most improbable romantic novel, he flew from the West Coast to New York to try to reconnect with this former wife.

Tina recalls the story that has been preserved in the family: "He literally threw himself—he was a very emotional, dramatic Irishman—and he just threw his body against the door of the convent. And he was shouting her name, 'Susan! Susan! Let me in!' "

But Susan was now Sister Mary Monica, and there was no turning back.

"Mother Ruth was very stern. It was very restricted in those days. She opened the door and said, 'You can't come in!' and then she slammed it shut. He was desperate, but he couldn't make contact with her. So he went back to Oregon and continued to pine for her over the years even though he stayed in his second marriage."

Over those same years, Sister Mary Monica became a revered figure in the convent. The current head of the community, Mother Madeleine Mary, thinks of her "as one of our saints." She had not been a religious person to begin with. She sowed her radical seeds. But she had had a number of difficulties in her life. She often found her way to the convent in the 1950s after she had met Mother Ruth.

This led to a conversion experience and her desire to have a time of her life to be alone, and that's when she joined the community.

"She was very loving. She really knew how to nurture people, and she did that a lot with her grandchildren. Tina came to her grandmother because everyone loved Grandma. And Grandma interceded for all of them."

Tina brought all this to her life-and-death crisis—a nonreligious upbringing; a decade of pluralism with the Unitarians; an intelligent, inquisitive husband who grew up a Theosophist but had now moved on to a synthesis of his own; and somewhere, hovering in the spiritual background, a grandmother who, more than forty-five years earlier, had left the everyday world to try to rescue her soul.

If Tina and Laurie were not religious in the traditional sense, it didn't mean they didn't seek for all the transcendent help they thought available. They found themselves praying more often and in different ways than they had ever prayed before.

Laurie admits that prayer had not been very important to him before.

"I'm not someone who prays. I don't pray regularly. Not because I'm not a spiritual person, because I am. But I feel personally I should only pray when it's really, really serious. And I don't like to pray for myself. But during this time I began to pray regularly for the first time in my life. When she was trying to keep the twins inside, I would say thanks for getting us through each day. I did that every single day. And then when I was jumping on the flight to Minneapolis to come out when she started to deliver, I prayed one more time. I just said, 'Thank you for getting us this far.'"

Not exactly storming the gates of heaven, perhaps, but an honest prayer of gratitude, one that does not go unheeded.

At the same time that Laurie was trying out this thing called prayer, Tina was going to the experts, literally to the professionals. The sisters make it their profession—the defining thing they do—to offer up the world to God in prayer. They do many other things in the world as well—teach, nurse, counsel, bring comfort—but the only two things they do every day are worship and pray, two sides of the same coin.

The sisters gather four times a day for worship, praying for specific requests each time. The requests come by mail, telephone, fax and, yes, by e-mail. They also come directly off the streets and by all other means imaginable. The requests are organized on a large bulletin board and are prayed for row by row, day by day, for as long as the need lasts, during both worship and personal prayer times.

Mother Madeleine Mary explains that evening prayers are typically devoted to intercession.

"Each day is different. Last night we prayed for the leaders of war-torn areas of the world, specifically for Kosovo. We also are praying for children right now. We might keep a theme for two months, but the specifics are never the same.

"And then our evening prayers have traditionally been for all those who will die tonight. We will introduce the theme and then the sisters will individually pray for the elderly who will die, and for those who will die from an act of violence in the city tonight, and then, perhaps, for any children who are dying tonight. And we will mention specific names when we know them. The master concept is that no ones dies without some prayer."

Whether you are a fundamentalist or a religious liberal or only vaguely spiritual, you have to be glad that there are women somewhere who intercede in this way each dark night of the world. As a matter of fact, Mother Madeleine Mary indicates that they are in relationship with a Lutheran community in Germany.

"We correspond frequently by e-mail, and one of their sisters recently wrote, 'When you go to sleep, we are praying, and when we go to sleep, you are praying.' So between us, we've got the world covered."

If one can cover the world, one can certainly take notice of the perils of two tiny babies, and the sisters did so enthusiastically. Is it any wonder that Tina wanted these women on her and her children's side?

The sisters have a system for spreading the word throughout the convent when there is an emergency situation requiring immediate prayer.

"If it's critical—someone going into emergency surgery or something—we have this little button on our telephone system for announcements. You can press that button and say, 'Everybody that is within hearing range of this phone, would you please pray for this person.' It's our hotline. But when Tina would call, we would just run through the house telling everyone."

Sometimes, instead of coming directly from Tina, the news came to the sisters from Lucy. Lucy is one of many associates of The Community of the Holy Spirit and lives near the convent, a few blocks off Central Park. She was a close friend of Tina's grandmother and through her became close to Sister Mary Monica's energetic granddaughter.

"Sister Mary Monica was a very important person in my life. She was an extraordinary woman and extraordinarily beautiful. She had a great influence on me. She healed something inside of me—through her generosity of spirit and the way she just accepted people. She was a woman of great kindness and true, deep modesty."

By the time Tina began visiting regularly during her college years, Sister Mary Monica's strength was declining. Tina and Lucy often took her out together, and in the process got to know and love each other.

"We took her grandmother to museums and to Wave Hill, a beautiful place, and to other places. I also worked with her in her small garden behind the convent."

Tina remembers that she could ask Lucy questions that she couldn't ask her grandmother.

"I could talk to her. I could just ask her if it was right to feel a certain way. I didn't feel she was judging me, and I was nervous sometimes to ask questions of Grandma because I didn't want to reveal how ignorant I was."

Tina's photography helped her in forming a bond with Lucy, as it had with the sisters. Lucy teaches at homeless shelters and recalls Tina's interest in her work.

"I'm a teacher, and Tina came and created a show of photographs of my students. I came to love Tina like a daughter."

She also watched the relationship between Tina and her grandmother grow. She knew something of Sister Mary Monica's hopes and fears for her granddaughter.

"She felt that Tina was restless and uncertain and uncommitted—which of course she was because she was young. I think she worried that because Tina was beautiful and from a family that had a lot, she could take certain things for granted in life. Her grandmother's fear was that she would stay sort of beautiful and scattered."

"Beautiful and scattered," like the heroines of a thousand novels. But Lucy and Sister Mary Monica sensed something deeper in Tina even in those early years.

"Even when she was young and scattered, she always showed the capacity for something much more. She has this enormous capacity to be changed, the capacity to feel blessed instead of cheated, the capacity to respond to people's kindness and to be kind in return."

Lucy joined in with the sisters in praying for and offering encouragement to Tina during the difficult weeks before and after the birth of Anna and Liam. But what exactly did they think they were accomplishing by praying? How was prayer in Manhattan going to have any effect on what was going on in Minneapolis?

These are not questions that can be answered definitively. One does not offer an explanation and then the questions go away, forever resolved. One *probes* such questions and offers ideas, reflections, experiences and intuitions, as does Mother Madeleine Mary.

"I think prayer is the power of love that is released into the world. It is a very strong power and should never be underestimated. It involves one's relationship with God. Prayer can activate healing and grace where people are open to those things. But where they cannot be received, they are not forced. God is gentle. I believe everyone who is open to healing is healed, but not everyone is cured."

She expands on this distinction between being healed and being cured in terms of her own immediate family.

"My youngest brother was hit by a cement truck. He died in surgery. He was not cured, but that experience in my own family's life has healed so much. His life means something. He did not die in vain."

Mother Madeleine Mary is careful to say that she does not think God caused her brother to die so as to teach the rest of the family a lesson. The accident happened, and God transformed it.

"God used the situation to help us feel that there was a power beyond this world that really did care about us—a power that wept with those who weep and is there to receive us in light when we die. It's not just a dead-end. And that's what I think prayer is about."

*   *   *

If that's what prayer is about, then Tina was in need of it, for she was doing a lot of weeping. She was confined to a hospital room for weeks on end with an overactive mind, great doubts about her own inner resources, an at best sketchy faith in any higher powers, and two threatened unborn infants. Her husband was far away, and some of those close to her were by nature more pessimistic than others.

Understandably, then, Tina spent a lot of time on the telephone. Laurie did his best to encourage her from Massachusetts. Lucy and the sisters did their best from New York. Mother Madeleine Mary knew there were no magic words to make all the pain and uncertainty go away.

"There's not much advice you can give in that kind of situation. I think Tina needed to tell her story and talk about her fears. She needed to know that somebody was there for her, and we were. She was feeling desperately alone and powerless. The world had been sort of an open field for her, where everything was at her fingertips, and now it had crashed in living color."

Mother Madeleine Mary also knew that something was at stake

here for Tina herself and for her entire family, not just for the twins, and that one had to be wise in how one approached such things.

"Prayer is a delicate matter. With human beings you don't want to try to dictate how things should be. When you are praying for healing, you also have to prepare the person to understand some-how that this experience can be a blessing no matter what the out-come. You have to meet the person where the person is. Tina was terrified. Her grandmother was no longer there to comfort her, but she needed to see that the prayers could enfold her, hug her, so that she could know God was with her. Because, you see, that's what God was to her at that point in her life, just the presence. We were trying to show that there was a God and that, no matter what, she was being accompanied in this pain."

Lucy believes the experience of being prayed for gave Tina a ground for hope that she had not found anywhere else.

"I think Tina began to understand what it meant to have people praying continually for her and that it was something that she could rest in. She began to feel the effects in her daily life."

The experience also taught Lucy some things about prayer and trying to help someone you love.

"You know, when Tina was at her mother's when the twins were struggling, she had a separate phone line put in. I wrote that number in pencil in my phonebook because I knew it was just temporary. After she came back to Massachusetts, I kept thinking I was going to erase it, but I couldn't. I realize now that I'm never going to erase it, because it reminds me of such an amazing time. I couldn't be there to help her, and I felt powerless. But she and the twins were con-stantly in my thoughts, and those thoughts were a kind of prayer."

When Lucy was actually speaking with Tina, rather than think-ing about her, she tried to be as encouraging as possible.

"I tried to speak about the upside of things with Tina. I said this was not a punishment for her but a kind of opportunity. She had a terrible need not to go in the direction of despair."

And yet, for all the prayers and support, despair is exactly where

Tina went in the hours before the twins were born.

"I had a complete breakdown. I couldn't take it anymore. All these people started calling me, and I had to turn the phone off because I couldn't handle talking to anybody. I didn't want any visitors. I just wanted to be left alone.

"I was very doped up on these drugs they gave me. They make you feel disembodied, completely out of it. I didn't have my husband with me, and even though my parents would try to come in every day, I felt totally adrift. I had no idea what was going to happen.

"I went crazy. I started hyperventilating. I called for the nurse and said, 'Debbie, please, can you come in here? I can't breathe! I feel like someone is sitting on my chest.' I told her, 'I think I'm dying.'"

Tina didn't die. In fact, after a night of medicated sleep, she awoke with a strange sense of well-being and new resolve.

"They gave me these sleeping pills—they were always giving me something—because they knew how stressed out I was. But the next morning I woke up and felt like a different person. I thought to myself, *All right, I can do this. I can get to twenty-eight weeks. I'm going to buckle down. I can get there. I have to.*"

Lucy had told her, "Tina, God does not give us more than we can handle." And now Tina felt she could handle whatever was to come.

She didn't get a chance to test her new resolve. The babies were born that night. Tina's contractions couldn't be stopped this time because the babies were in distress. Further use of drugs carried the risk of brain damage for the children. When her water broke, there was no longer any decision to be made. They wheeled her into delivery.

"I was holding one of the nurse's hands—it was either Sandy or Jeanette. All I could see were their eyes. Then I saw Dr. Hoekstra for the first time. My mom's doctor was doing the delivery. There were also an anesthesiologist, a couple of nurses to assist the doctors, two NICU nurses and I think two respiratory therapists. My mother counted sixteen people in the room, counting me."

Whatever calmness Tina had felt earlier in the day carried over into the delivery.

"I felt like there was this entity, this power, this spirit that was there that I gave myself up to. It was like I trusted. I felt this trust in something. I can't put my finger on it, but I felt everything was okay. Everything was going to work out."

This was not the first time in Tina's family that someone felt surrounded by something larger than herself in a time of acute danger.

"My parents were in a very serious car accident a few years ago. The car rolled four times. My mother's neck was broken in three places. She had very serious injuries. She told me later, 'After the accident I felt this incredible love coming from all around that just enveloped me.' It was the first time I ever heard her say anything like that. My mother's a skeptic, and I know what that feels like. I don't want to misrepresent her. My mom's complicated. But it sounded like she felt there might be somebody out there watching her and loving her."

Sister Mary Monica would not have doubted that the "somebody out there" who surrounded her daughter after her car crashed was also the one who enveloped her daughter's daughter when she was about to deliver her endangered children.

"I definitely feel that I was guided through this experience. I feel I got strength from knowing deep down, intuitively, that someone or something was behind this."

٭   ٭   ٭

Laurie was called when the births seemed imminent. He spent the night trying to find the earliest plane to Minneapolis, but he was not there at three in the morning when the twins finally came.

Delivering twins is a risky proposition, especially when they are born at twenty-five weeks. The babies had to be manipulated in the uterus to get them in position for birth.

"It was like he was changing a tire. They were like slippery little

fish in there. They were so little. Anna came out first, and I couldn't
look. I just squeezed those hands that I was holding so tightly."

Anna was born at 3:18 a.m. and weighed one pound seven
ounces. Liam followed three minutes later at one pound eight
ounces. Tina couldn't look at her children. Would they be alive?
Would they be whole?

Then she heard Liam cry. She also heard her mother's voice.

"My mom said, 'You have to look. You have to look. Turn your
head.' I was scared, but I heard him crying, and I turned my head
and saw this body with these arms and legs waving. He was so little,
but you could see this life—he was so alive!"

Tina had not expected this.

"I thought they were going to look pretty bad. I didn't expect to
see that life! That fighting spirit already. That little fighting life,
right there. God, it was just so vivid."

Tina wasn't the only one who felt some trepidation about first
looking at her children. Laurie, who arrived later that morning,
recalled a scene from Tolstoy's great novel *Anna Karenina* and
wondered how he would react when he first saw the twins.

"The main character's wife has a baby, and he goes in to see it,
expecting to be enraptured by this baby. Instead he sees this lardy,
messy, screaming thing, and he's shocked by his revulsion, though
he eventually comes to love it. I really wanted to look at these
babies and love them, but I know that sometimes it's not immediate. It takes a little while for the father to warm up to them, and I
didn't know how to do it."

Laurie found, however, that in this case life superseded art.

"When I came into the room, it was hard not to see all the technology there, but I just felt this incredible, strong wave of empathy
for these two babies immediately. There was absolutely no revulsion at all. It was simply, 'These are mine.' I just felt love for them.
It was an earthly love and divine love at the same time. Maybe love
is the thing that more than anything else connects the earthly and
the divine."

*   *   *

The lives of Anna and Liam changed many people, beginning with their parents but moving out in ever widening rings to include others. The first person included beyond the parents was Tina's mother.

"My mom feels like she delivered those babies. It was like she went through it herself. She says it was the most powerful thing that ever happened in her life, and she's had a number of powerful experiences. It was also the most difficult thing she's ever gone through. But it's wonderful. She can't believe the gift they are."

Tina can't talk about her mother and the delivery without crying. It is clear that one of the many things that has been affected by Anna and Liam is Tina's relationship with her mother.

"There's no doubt that seeing where they came from and what happened and what could have happened made them special. They are such a gift and miracle that she will probably always hold them closer than she would have otherwise. They're from me and I'm from her and she loves them so much, like she does all her grand-children. But because of the odds against them and the strength we all needed to give each other, it made a huge impact on her life. She's a changed woman."

Tina did not see Dr. Hoekstra again until five days after the delivery. She tried to thank him.

"I was excited to see him. I remember walking up to him in the lobby of the NICU and saying, 'Thank you so much for what you've done.' And he immediately tried to deflect any credit. He took me aside into a room and said, 'It wasn't me. I do the best I can, but I want you to know that actually it's in God's hands.'"

Nothing in Tina's past had prepared her for this kind of response.

"That had a huge impact on me. I had been feeling that way but hadn't been able to articulate it until that moment. And to hear it from a doctor! So many doctors think they *are* God, and here's a doctor who *prays* to God!"

Tina also wasn't the only one impressed by Dr. Hoekstra's faith. Laurie, whose conception of God is quite generalized, found something both helpful and believable in Dr. Hoekstra's more specific understanding.

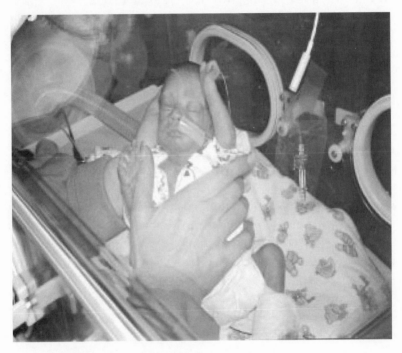

Liam momentarily off his oxygen at two weeks

"One thing that was incredible in the NICU was Dr. Hoekstra's faith. To have somebody who was both an excellent doctor and who talked that way, well . . . Some of the other doctors would try to be positive, but Dr. Hoekstra was different. He would say, 'These kids are going to be good. I really have a good feeling about them.' And we knew he wasn't just saying it to sound optimistic."

They also knew that such an approach was not universally admired in the NICU.

"It was clear that some of the doctors felt he went too far in that direction. They felt he was just trying to make the parents feel good. But that wasn't it, and it wasn't just optimism that helped sustain us. It was his faith, and the fact that his faith gave him some kind of intuitive knowledge—a vision—that was more than just hopeful. It was not presumptive. There was more to it."

Tina adds, "What's wrong with putting the parents at ease a little bit? It was a very generous thing to do."

✻   ✻   ✻

The moment of delivery is usually a mountaintop experience. The days and weeks immediately after often signal a return to the plains, sometimes into the valley. Life was already extremely difficult for Tina—physically, psychologically and spiritually—in the weeks before the twins were born. Despite the tremendous relief of seeing them come into the world healthy, she would find the first months of their life almost more than she could handle.

"I had a violent allergic reaction to the morphine or whatever they gave me during delivery. I was scratching myself raw for days and days. The pain was outrageous."

Anna and Liam's birth at twenty-five weeks gave them a huge advantage over twenty-two and twenty-three weekers. A great deal of development happens in a few weeks in the life of the unborn, and the twins were spared many of the major threats to the greatly premature. But they were not spared everything, especially not Liam.

"They were both on ventilators for three weeks. Anna finally pulled her tube out, and Dr. Hoekstra said we would leave it out and see how she did. She did fine and never lost weight and just kept improving. We would even stop asking about her because she was always fine. But Liam just struggled."

In the early days, when the possibility of major disabilities still existed, Tina's response indicated a kind of growth in her that could not have been predicted a few months before. Lucy could detect it over the telephone.

"There was such a change in Tina. It was phenomenal. At one point there was the possibility that one of the children might be retarded. I was rallying to say something uplifting to her. And she said, 'Of course, whatever this child is, we'll be able to take care of it.' That's a big difference in Tina."

Tina expresses it similarly in her own words. When Laurie says how lucky they feel to have two wonderful, healthy children, Tina makes clear that the children's health is not what makes them valuable.

"We would have loved them regardless. I mean we would have totally loved them. We had been prepared for what could have happened, and I know I could have loved them that way—with cerebral palsy or blindness or whatever else."

Tina and Laurie did not have to deal with blindness, but they did have to battle through Liam's respiratory and intestinal problems. He was in the hospital for three months, on steroids intermittently. His lungs were weak and vulnerable.

Liam's most difficult problem, however, was keeping food in his stomach. He had what one doctor called the worst case of reflux in a preemie that he had ever seen. He vomited regularly, possibly as a consequence of his breathing difficulties.

"He was on six different medications. Four times a day he underwent an inhalant treatment to keep his lungs open. They had to put an NG tube—a nasogastric tube—through his nose and into his stomach in an attempt to get him some nourishment."

This went on for months. After Liam had been in the hospital for six months—during which time Anna came home, and he bounced around to different units—Tina and Laurie were told it was time to take him home. As much as they had looked forward to that day, they didn't feel ready.

"They said, 'You have to go home now. You just have to do it.' But we felt like, *Wait a second! He's not ready to go!* But they took out the NG tube and sent him home on oxygen and a host of medications. But once at home, he wouldn't eat. He wouldn't breast-feed or bottle-feed. He would throw everything up. We were up with him all night for three or four nights in a row. We were absolutely freaking out. We were a wreck."

They took Liam back to the hospital, and some of the nurses greeted them with, "We were wondering how long it would take for you to be back." Liam stayed another ten days and then went home again, not really any better than before.

*   *   *

The days at Tina's mom's were very difficult. Liam continued to throw up constantly. Dr. Hoekstra recruited one of the hospital nurses to go and lend a hand. Lois was a great help to Tina in many different ways, but finally they decided they had to take the twins back to Massachusetts.

The airline wasn't so sure. Tina called two months ahead of time to appraise it of the situation and then made reservations when they decided it was time to go.

"Then twenty-four hours before we were to fly back, the fellow who is the head of arrangements for special situations called and said we couldn't fly. He said the oxygen tank situation wouldn't work. We said we were coming anyway, and he said, 'If you try to get on that plane, I will have you apprehended by the police. Don't even try.'"

Not exactly customer service at its best, but sometimes it pays to go beyond the first bureaucrat who says no.

"We called Lois, whose neighbor worked for the airline. Within three or four hours we were on the phone with the chief dispatcher. He is a fantastic guy who just out of his own kindness decided we were going to get home. He put us in first class and had the fire department escort us on and off the plane. At the boarding gate we think we spotted the guy who had said we would be arrested lurking in the background, and he was really upset.

"The chief dispatcher also had the flight designated a life-saving flight, so we got priority in taking off and landing. He had them patch through to Mayo Clinic so we could have medical consulta-

tion if we needed it, and he had them alert hospitals along the way
so they could be prepared just in case. And to finish it off, there was
a telegram from him waiting for us at the other end to make sure
that we had made it okay."

Tina knows that a man helping with a plane flight was not the
most important thing in their children's lives at that time, but she
calls it "another act of goodness." It was one in a long series of such
acts, and there were many more unexpected ones to come.

Tina and Laurie and the twins returned to Great Barrington, a
small, picturesque town in western Massachusetts. They had moved
there from New York just over two years before but still did not
know many people. There were no more doctors on call, no more
nurses, no mother, no parents' home. There was only Tina, Anna, a
still sick Liam and a supportive Laurie, who nonetheless had to go
to work. It was a recipe for exhaustion tinged with despair.

The single most difficult part of taking care of the twins was
Liam's nasogastric tube. There is no way of verifying that it is in the
stomach, so one has to gauge in advance how much tube to feed
into the nose so that when you stop, the end will be in the stomach.
It was not only hard on Liam, but, as Tina remembers, it created
tension between her and Laurie because of how difficult it was to
get it right.

"It was hard between us because of the things we had to do to
Liam—getting that lousy tube down his nose."

The story of one night can stand for many. Laurie recalls a night-
mare evening when they simply couldn't get the tube into Liam's
stomach.

"We tried seven or eight times, and he just screamed each time
we tried. It was so traumatic. We couldn't get it down. Finally we
stopped and said, 'We can't do this.' We called one of the pediatricians in town, and she came over. She's an Ivy League-trained doctor. She said, 'Oh yeah, I know how to do this.' Then she said, 'You
just measure from here to here.' But we knew she was wrong
because we had been trained in how to measure and what she said

wasn't right. Nevertheless, we finally got the tube down with her. Then she left the house, and Liam immediately threw it up. We had to start all over."

*   *   *

From time to time Dr. Hoekstra called Tina to see how everything was going. He could tell she was going downhill. She needed help, but help seemed distant. It turned out that help was just a phone call away.

Dr. Hoekstra knew that Tina and Laurie did not go to church. But he asked Tina, "If you did go to church back there, which one do you think you would go to?" She hesitated for a moment and then, perhaps with her grandmother in mind, said, "Maybe the Episcopal church in Stockbridge, the next town up the road from here. I don't know the name of it." She and Laurie had gone to a funeral there once, and it seemed as good a choice as any.

Dr. Hoekstra hung up the phone and called information. He asked whether there was an Episcopal church in Stockbridge, Massachusetts, and was given a number. He called the number, hoping for the best, and that's what he got.

"I introduced myself and asked for the pastor of the church. The voice on the other end said, 'That would be me.' I explained the situation. He understood immediately and just picked up the ball. I never talked to him again after that."

The voice on the other end was John Tarrant, rector of St. Paul's Episcopal Church. He and his wife, Pat, had come to serve at the church only a few years earlier. He was impressed that a doctor from Minnesota cared enough about the total well-being of a patient half a continent away to try to track down an unknown church to see "how they could walk this walk together."

"I've been ordained for fifteen years, and this was the first time anyone had called from that distance with concern about someone local. It was especially impressive that it was a doctor with a vision for people beyond just the physical."

Reverend Tarrant called Tina that same afternoon and then came over to see what he could do. He found her open to receiving help, though somewhat mystified that people who didn't know her would want to give it.

"They needed hands. They didn't need money. They needed hands to help them with these two little ones. And that was something folks were able to provide. I went through the church that Sunday looking for volunteers. Different people could do different things. One woman didn't think she could help with the babies, but she could go over and iron and do dishes or make a meal. I was impressed with how people used their imaginations to figure out ways they could help."

One person recruited another, and in a very short time there was what seemed like a small army of volunteers ready to do battle. At the center, coordinating the whole, was Tessa, a young woman with a gift for organization and a desire to serve. Tessa made many of the initial arrangements for people to come so that Tina wouldn't be overwhelmed with phone calls. A calendar was also set up over the diaper-changing table where people could write in their names for future dates.

When people would come into the home, they often knew what to do and would set about doing it. They tried to leave Tina free from the need to talk with the volunteers so that she could do the many things she had to do. Often one volunteer would be upstairs with one baby while Tina or another volunteer was downstairs with the other.

Pat Tarrant was one of those who did whatever came to hand.

"In the beginning I would go over twice a week. I'd try to give her a real block of time, four or five hours, to do whatever she needed me to do. Sometimes I'd vacuum or do the dishes. Often we didn't even ask her what to do. We'd just go in and see what had to be done and do it. She could leave to run errands or get a break, but she would always call after about thirty minutes to see how things were going."

Pat spent much of her time, however, rocking Liam. He was often discontented or in pain, still vomiting frequently and still burdened with his nasogastric tube.

"I would rock Liam for as much as three hours at a time. I would rock him and pray. I would just talk to God about Liam. 'Relieve his pain, God. Settle him down, comfort him.' I would also talk to Liam about God. I would talk to him about God's love for him and about Jesus. I talked to him as if he could understand, and I found that it not only helped Liam but gave me the kind of peace I needed to be able to do what I had to do.

"Otherwise I would have been fretting. I would have thought *Oh, he's fussing, he's fussing. What's wrong with him?* Instead I tried to let go and put him in God's hands. And, you know, he was very content to be in my arms. It was so wonderful when he went to sleep. Just for his peace. He was so beautiful."

It is telling that Pat Tarrant reports *finding* peace in the very act of trying to *give* peace to someone else. It touches on some fundamental truth about the nature of human beings and of the universe. That which you give away in love comes back to you for your own good.

Her husband touches on the same concept when he talks about Tessa and the blessing that the opportunity to help Tina and Laurie was for her.

"It was just a peace that came into her life. Tessa and her husband had only been in the church a few months. It was a peace that came into her life during a very important time, and it gave her the opportunity to help."

At the beginning, Tina did not understand that people would be willing, even eager, to help someone they didn't know without being paid. She recalls her bewilderment.

"John Tarrant came over within an hour after he had talked to Dr. Hoekstra. He said, 'Tell me your story.' After I told him, he said, 'I'd like to help.' My reaction was, 'Help? What do you mean?' I didn't understand the concept of volunteering and church community and helping in that way. I couldn't get over it."

Reverend Tarrant remembers the conversation.

"She just didn't understand it at first. She offered to pay the people. I had to tell her, 'Tina, that's not the deal. These people would be insulted if you offered them money. You'll have your day to give back, but this is your day to receive.'"

As well as not fully understanding other people's impulse to help, Tina was uncomfortable at first with her family becoming public figures.

"Suddenly we had all these people in our house. We were very private people before. Now we felt like our life was a spectacle. We had these two children on oxygen and would take walks in the neighborhood. We live in a town of seven hundred people, and everybody in town seemed to know about us even before we got back from Minneapolis. Suddenly our lives were wide open for everyone to see. For me it was hard to adjust to because I wanted fiercely to protect my children, and I wanted everything to appear happy and rosy to everyone on the outside."

Tina didn't know how to accept help or exactly what people could do. Lucy offered her some wisdom.

"Tina said to me at one point, 'How am I going to let people come over? How am I going to tell them what to do? I can't just ask them to do laundry!' And I said to her, 'Well, just imagine, Tina, if it was the reverse, and you found out about a woman who had premature babies who were still at risk and who was overwhelmed. Wouldn't you want to run over and do something for her?' And she said, 'Yeah, okay.'"

Throughout the entire ordeal Tina was blessed with compassionate women coming into her life who shared their experience and wisdom with her when she most needed it.

❊   ❊   ❊

Perhaps no one took more pure joy in helping than a neighbor of the Tarrants, Pat Donovan. Pat is not a member of St. Paul's, but she can't resist an opportunity to help someone out. She has an almost insatiable hunger for helping, and if children are involved, she becomes ravenous.

Pat grew up north of Boston, and that fact is stamped unmistakably in her speech. A short woman in her late fifties or early sixties, she has a perpetual, gnomish youthfulness about her. Pat smiles easily and often, and she exudes an infectious energy and love of life and of people.

Like Tina and Laurie, Pat was fairly new to the area and feeling a bit directionless.

"The chance to help was a wonderful thing for me. I had only lived in Stockbridge a short time, and where I lived before for thirty-one years, I was very connected for volunteering and friends. I didn't have that here, and I was kind of lonesome and purposeless. I don't even have any grandkids. Isn't that awful! So when I hitched up with the twins, I felt like I got reconnected to the universe. The first time Liam went to sleep in my arms, I was home."

Feeling at home in the universe—through serving. This is an intriguing phenomenon.

Like everyone else, Pat was concerned about Liam.

"I never worried about Anna. I could feel her wiriness and the strength in her little body. But Liam cried a lot and was uncomfortable, and that kept everyone nervous. We were all dedicated to getting Liam to sleep. And since he had so many bosoms to rest on, we were pretty successful."

One of Pat's strategies for getting Liam to sleep was singing.

"Tina has this lovely lullaby tape. I would just sort of croon to him."

Tina remembers it differently.

"At first I thought she was crazy. I could hear her over the intercom down in the kitchen. We have this mobile upstairs with all these little animals, like a lion and a seal. She was singing to Liam one day and making a noise like each animal would make. When I heard her down in the kitchen, I thought, *Oh my God, this woman is out of her mind.* I adore her. She's a great person."

The admiration is mutual. Pat sees Tina like one of those animals on the mobile and gives Laurie credit for being a rare kind of husband under these circumstances.

"We were in crisis over there. The whole thing was actually a rescue mission. Tina and Laurie were working like dogs. Tina was exhausted, but her adrenaline was marvelous. She was like a lioness over those babies. She was such a good force.

"And Laurie was so cooperative with her. He would come home and say, 'Okay, what do you want me to do?'—the minute he walked in the door. Some husbands would have been frightened by it all—alarms going off at night, not getting good sleep. But he was always trying his best, and I loved him for that. You could really say he was kind of noble throughout. I saw that he was some classy guy."

Perhaps a dozen people volunteered over a period of about four months, until Tina and Laurie hired an au pair to live in and help with the kids. Tina's amazement that there were people in the world like this may itself be somewhat amazing, but her fundamental question is a valid one. Why *would* people complicate their own lives in this way for people with whom they have no previous connection?

John Tarrant's answer has to do with the nature of the church generally and his hopes for his own church specifically. In simple terms, he feels people can do what the people of his church did because their lives have been transformed by the example of and their faith in Jesus.

"Last week's Gospel reading was from the end of the book of John. He tells of Jesus' death and resurrection and of the story of Thomas, who cannot believe without actually seeing and touching Jesus himself. The text says, 'Blessed are those who have not seen and yet have come to believe.'

"Then John says there are many other stories of what Jesus did that John hasn't put down. He has recorded only *some* of the stories in the Gospel. And he says, 'I put down *these* stories so that you may come to believe that Jesus is the Christ, the son of the living God, and that through believing you may have life.'

"So I reflected on that in my sermon—on what that means, and how that is what I'm about and what I'd like our church to be about—a place that knows and understands that Jesus is the Messiah, the son of the living God, and that through believing you can have life. If we present that, we have done our job. Then as people grow into that, they'll change the rules. Because if you believe that, if you embrace it, you can't help but be transformed. And as you're transformed, the world around you is transformed."

Tina and Laurie do not fully understand the Gospel of John or the language John Tarrant uses in discussing it. But they do testify to having been transformed.

Pat Donovan's answer to why she wanted to help is much less theological and more tangible but not really all that different. She can't understand why anyone would *not* want to help.

"Imagine somebody just needing you to love a baby! That's a terrific request. It got to be pretty good duty, especially when they opened up the front porch. Liam loved going outdoors. He would change as soon as he was out there. We'd sit on the porch and listen to the linden leaves tinkling, and you had this little baby snuggled against you. Yes, that was nice duty. And it was a measure of progress. The season had changed, summer came, and there was new hope."

There was also the added benefit for Pat of extending her family, of finding a new group of people to love.

"There was a lot of purpose and satisfaction in helping and then getting to love the babies and their parents. It was like getting some wonderful new relatives. You weren't kept separate from the family. They just brought you right in."

One last reason for helping slips out of Pat.

"I remember how scary it was to be a new mother."

When John Tarrant talks about his church, he envisions God

becoming flesh in Christ as the model for Christ becoming flesh in men and women and thereby transforming themselves and the world. Pat Donovan is a concrete example of that abstract principle, as were all the other volunteers, and the nuns, and Lucy, and Dr. Hoekstra.

Sister Mary Monica would have understood this. Tina and Laurie did not—at least not in these terms. But they knew they had come into contact with something fundamental and powerful, and that their own lives were changed.

Tina is overwhelmed by the concrete expressions of love they received from so many different quarters.

"I learned so much about the capacity to love. And it was such a humbling experience to receive so much love and help from people—doctors and nurses and friends and family. It changed me forever. I will never ever take any of that for granted anymore—take life for granted. I don't know. I feel like I want to make up for it for the rest of my life."

Experiencing this practical love from everyday people became for Tina and Laurie the most powerful argument they had encountered for the existence of God. For Tina it was the best answer to the "Why do they want to help?" question.

"There was this entity that was providing strength and hope and love from people I don't even know. And I kept thinking, 'Where is this coming from?' That was one of the main things that made me feel like there must be a God behind all these people. One of the most profound things for me in the experience of my children's births was all these people, including my mother, who helped us and showed love and compassion and care and guidance. I felt like there must be a God. Because this is what it's about."

Laurie had similar thoughts.

"To me there's a very strong connection between the ability to get through something like this and love. There's a well-worn phrase, 'God is love.' And the thing that gets us through is the love that you receive in such circumstances. It's not something you expect."

Typically, Tina thinks back to something from her grandmother.

"Grandma gave me this little piece of paper a long time ago from somebody in the fourteenth century or sometime that said, 'God is good.' Only *good* was spelled *gode,* so it said, 'God is gode.' You could see a kind of equation there, like the words *God* and *good* are the same thing. As though, if it's good, it's from God, and if it's from God, then it's good."

Reverend Tarrant couldn't have said it any better.

Because she has received love, Tina has a tremendous urge to give love. This too is an eternal principle.

"I feel like giving more love to the people around me—acts of kindness and love and compassion. I want to give back. When you receive so much, it's a lesson. You want to give back. I want to volunteer more and do acts of goodness, but I'm tied up now with the twins. But I'm giving back as a friend and a daughter and, hopefully, as a wife and mother.

"You know, when people said they were praying for me and for the twins, it made me want to cry. I thought, *No one has ever prayed for me in my life.* Since then, I've discovered people who have been praying for me from the day I was born. Now I pray for other people all the time."

Tina's entire sense about people and the purpose of life has changed.

"I think so differently about people. Before this experience it was easier for me not to expect good things from people, to always see the cup as half-empty and to expect bad things to happen and expect people not to be good. Now that is changed. I'm much more willing to accept and love and give the benefit of the doubt. Life is not worth wasting your time being angry, bitter, hateful, vengeful— there's so much more. It's all about love and being generous and hopeful and happy and spreading that as much as possible."

Tina and Laurie were, by common wisdom, unlucky. They had a very difficult time getting pregnant. She suffered a variety of painful ailments during the pregnancy. They agonized over the possibility of losing their children if they came too soon, as they threatened to do. She endured an extremely difficult hospitalization to bring the children to delivery at twenty-five weeks, and then they struggled for weeks and months to coax the children to health. This seeming bad luck, however, changed for the better their view of God, of themselves, of other people and of what life is about. One would not choose the kind of trouble Tina and Laurie have seen, or wish it for someone else. But one can begin to see how some trouble can work for good.

There seems to be, somewhere near the center of reality, an openness to suffering. Jews and Christians worship a God who suffers, who Christians believe joined with his creation in the person of Jesus Christ in order to suffer with us for the priceless purpose of making us right with God. Even those uninterested in religious faith usually allow for some link between pain and character.

Tina attributes to her suffering a profound change in who she is and how she sees life.

"I feel like through this experience I have lost my innocence in a way. I had been living in a dream world. I had never had to suffer. Before the problems started, my biggest concern was, 'Should I get a side-by-side stroller or a front-back stroller?' Or, 'Should I paint the nursery green or blue?' Then suddenly the question was, 'Will my babies be blind? Will they live?' It's incredible how your perspective changes.

"Nothing bad had ever happened to me. I've lived a charmed, happy, very fortunate life. And I feel like I now am part of a larger community of those who have suffered. Lucy said you become part of a different community once you have gone through this kind of suffering. It's as though you cross over a line and you're no longer naïve. She had suffered a great deal in her life. And now I understand. I feel like we've been so lucky. But I also feel like there's no going back to what I was before. You can still enjoy life and be light and happy, but there's this gravity to life that you didn't know about."

Laurie is not comfortable with this way of putting it.

"I prefer not to look at it that way. I don't want to see myself as part of a community of sufferers, because there's so much joy in the world. I prefer not to say I'm a sufferer. I'm just a human being who's trying to do the best I can. I feel quite humbled by it all—by life."

Perhaps the difference is that Laurie sees suffering and joy as mutually exclusive, whereas Tina and Lucy find they sometimes go hand in hand. Mere psychological happiness is driven out by suffering, but suffering can be the very soil of spiritual joy.

When the au pair, Franzie, came to live with them, the time for the volunteers ended. They were needed for a season, and they met the need, and then went on to other things. This is how it should be.

Liam continued to have problems. He was scheduled for a major operation that would have wrapped part of his stomach around his esophagus to stop the vomiting. It potentially would have had life-long consequences. But after extensive testing, the doctor decided to wait.

Waiting was hard and Liam seemed no better, so the surgery was scheduled again. But the doctor examined Liam and said, "He looks good to me. He's gaining weight. You guys are too close to this." So they took him home once more, and five days later he stopped vomiting. After months of struggle, the ordeal was over. Now he is as healthy as his sister Anna, and all the ordeals are the normal ones for curious, energy-draining twins.

*   *   *

Sometimes life seems a series of circles—circles of endless repetition if it is going nowhere, circles of completion if it is. Tina's grandmother completed her own circle and initiated others, some that seem to have come to completion in turn, and others that are still in process.

She even completed a kind of circle with her former husband.

They had written letters over the years but had never seen each other again. He had gotten married for a third time, to a friend of Tina's mother who was thirty-five years younger than he was. Tina was visiting him in Oregon during her freshman year of college.

"We were all sitting around the table, and the phone rang. My grandfather, who was eighty-five at this time, got up and went into the other room to answer the phone. Suddenly we hear this shout, 'Susan!' They hadn't spoken together in thirty-five years. I guess she figured it was time for a call.

"Later he arranged through a cousin of mine who was at Columbia to go see her. So they had this wonderful reunion in New York when both of them were in their eighties. Eventually Grandpa went into a nursing home. He never changed. He was making passes at his twenty-five-year-old nurse when he was ninety.

"I was with my family at the ranch in Montana when we got word that Grandpa had died. We all caravaned immediately to Oregon. Grandma flew in. She spoke at his funeral. It was such an amazing thing. It was this full circle, with this beautiful love that still came out of her and never ended. She was such a graceful woman."

A graceful woman—that is, a woman full of grace. At one level, grace suggests a kind of dignified ease of conduct. At a deeper level, grace is getting and giving better than we deserve. If there is, in fact, love at the heart of the universe, it expresses itself most clearly and necessarily in the grace it extends to us.

Sister Mary Monica died in 1993. She died with certain hopes for her family as yet unfulfilled. The Community of the Holy Spirit is not a proselytizing order. As Lucy says, "It is their manner of life that is attractive, not any dogma they might teach." Tina and her grandmother did not have long conversations about God or faith or the meaning of life.

"My grandmother understood that we had not been brought up in a religious household, and she didn't try to convince me of anything. That's not how my grandmother wanted to teach me. Besides sides, she felt she was grappling too. She didn't have this perfect

Anna and Liam at fourteen months

certainty. She was dealing with what she called her 'meanies,' things within her that she wanted to change. It was a process for her as well."

And yet, Tina always knew that her grandmother had something that no one else in the family had.

"Even though we never really talked directly about it, I knew that there were answers that she had to give me. It's hard to express. It was an intangible understanding for me that there was a source of light that was being shone to me and to my family—that there is a God, in whatever form. And finally understanding *that*, along with really feeling people's prayers, is what carried me through."

A grandmother's hopes were finally fulfilled and another circle completed in a small chapel in upstate New York. The Community of the Holy Spirit has a retreat house in Brewster. In the August heat friends and family and adopted family gathered there for a baptism—for three baptisms, to be precise.

It was a time of joy and celebration for many different reasons. The sisters came from the city, including Sister Mary Christabel, Tina's grandmother's closest friend in the convent; the volunteers from St. Paul's came from Stockbridge; family members came from various parts of the country and the world. John Tarrant helped officiate, as did the priest who had counseled Tina and Laurie before their marriage. The same priest, speaking of circles, had also given Sister Mary Monica her last rites before she died—with Tina and Lucy present. Now he was helping to baptize her grandchildren.

The significance of this event was lost on no one. Mother Madeleine Mary saw it as the fulfillment of a grandmother's faithful prayers. She also provided a final nudge to complete another circle.

"I was really touched when Tina called and said that she thought Grandma would want the children baptized and that she wanted them baptized in our house. And I said, 'And what about you?' Her first response was, 'Well, I don't want to take away from the baptism of the children.' And I said, 'I don't think your grandmother would see it that way.'"

No, Grandmother would not have seen it that way. And neither, in time, did Tina. She decided to be baptized along with Anna and Liam.

"The community was thrilled—it was like Tina had come home! Her grandmother was up there saying, 'Finally, yes!' It was the completion of her wish, of all the prayers she had prayed over the years. But, you know, it wouldn't have happened if those people from that parish hadn't done what they did. They were wonderful."

Pat Donovan, who was not a member of that parish but simply a neighbor with a servant's heart, found herself in tears.

"During the ceremony I started crying almost uncontrollably. Here were all these people, including Tina's sister from England, and the Tarrants, and the people who had volunteered, and all those beautiful nuns who had really prayed. And in the center of the room were the babies, which was very good. We were actually surrounding them. I thought to myself that prayer had been rewarded, and that Tina and Laurie's efforts were rewarded. And then we sang this song that declared that every baby, every person, is a miraculous child of God.

"Here were the babies in the middle of the room. And when we started singing, they looked around at all of us. Things had come full circle."

Lucy has a different metaphor.

"I first saw it at the requiem service held for Sister Mary Monica back in 1993. I looked at Tina, and she had this steady, solid, beautiful face. She was so present—to the death, to the service, to everything around her. I thought to myself, *The mantle has been passed on.* She has always had this great capacity for generosity of spirit, and to be fully open to the spiritual. And now I think she has the faith. The mantle from her grandmother has been passed."

Some circles have been completed. The arcs of others are not yet closed. All because of two small babies born before their time.

CHAPTER SIX

"WON'T YOU EVEN TRY?" ONE DOCTOR'S THOUGHTS ABOUT THOSE BORN TOO SOON

"Life is a lot more precious once you see it."

DR. RON HOEKSTRA

"The fear of the LORD is the beginning of knowledge."

PROVERBS 1:7

For parents, the birth of a severely premature child is a life-defining event that changes all things. For the doctors and other medical people who take care of these babies, the event is common-place but no less life defining. They make a thousand everyday decisions that are purely medical and routine for every one that has important ethical or moral implications.

But those one-in-a-thousand decisions strike at the heart of who they are as individuals and what we are as a society. They not only raise questions about life and death but about who should be given a chance to live and who should not, about when treatment is for the good of the baby and when it is doing no one any good, about how to tell people things they most do not want to hear, about what kind of life is worth living, and about who should decide such a thing. These are only a few of the questions faced daily in the high-tech world of the NICU—questions for which there are no high-tech answers.

*　　*　　*

In our society the time of greatest risk for any child is the moment when his or her existence is first detected. We have granted ourselves the power to end life at the very moment it begins. The child must immediately be deemed desirable because society has already deemed it expendable. If the idea of the child appeals to the mother, the adventure of life can continue—if not, it may, for no additonal reason, be ended.

Those who pass that initial barrier must then get to the point of viability, that shadowy line before which life outside the womb is deemed impossible or too risky or too expensive. The next big questions after "Do you want this child?" are "How early is too early? How small is too small?"

Medical science cannot answer these questions alone. Everyone realizes that the risks increase as the gestational age and size decrease. People disagree about how much risk and how much imperfection is acceptable. We used to hear a lot of talk about viability and the third trimester of pregnancy. Medical advances have made much of that talk obsolete.

In the early 1970s not many children could be expected to live if born before twenty-eight weeks. By the early 1980s the critical point had moved to twenty-seven weeks and then to twenty-six. Today there is wide consensus that every effort should be made to resuscitate infants born at twenty-four weeks of pregnancy or after.

Not everyone agrees, however. Shelley, one of B. J.'s nurses, recalls listening with shock at a conference where a doctor described the case of an infant born at twenty-seven weeks, far further along than the babies we have described. The baby did not need a ventilator but did require what is known as a CPAP—continuous positive airway pressure. This is oxygen or a mixture of air and oxygen flowing into the lungs, usually through two small prongs in the baby's nose, which keeps the tiny air sacs open between breaths. It is a very common procedure and not at all extreme or invasive. The doctor at the conference, however, said those treating the infant believed it was the parents' choice whether to supply this help. The parents decided against it, and the baby was allowed to die. Shelley shook her head, "I couldn't have taken care of that baby knowing that could happen."

If there is consensus that twenty-four weeks is, for the time being, a reasonable point at which most infants should be given every chance to live, there is disagreement about what efforts should be made for those who come just before. Past evidence of low survival rates and high incidence of long-term disabilities for babies born at twenty-three weeks or before make many doctors reluctant to act aggressively on the part of any infant born before twenty-four weeks.

The practice of which Dr. Hoekstra is a part has decided not to draw the lines so indelibly that "little warriors," as Bennie called B. J., have no chance of taking their shot at life. They resuscitate all infants born at twenty-three weeks or later, and they have the long-term data to defend their choice.

But if one resuscitates at twenty-three weeks, then what about at twenty-two? Most people think that the lungs—machines and drugs notwithstanding—are simply not far enough developed anatomically to support life outside the uterus at twenty-two weeks. Normally, neonatologists are not even called to attend deliveries of infants born at this age or before. When parents insist, Dr. Hoekstra's practice makes every effort on behalf of the infant, making clear to the parents that survival is very unlikely, and significant long-term problems for the few who do survive are to be expected.

Yet even the twenty-two weekers can make their bid for life. You

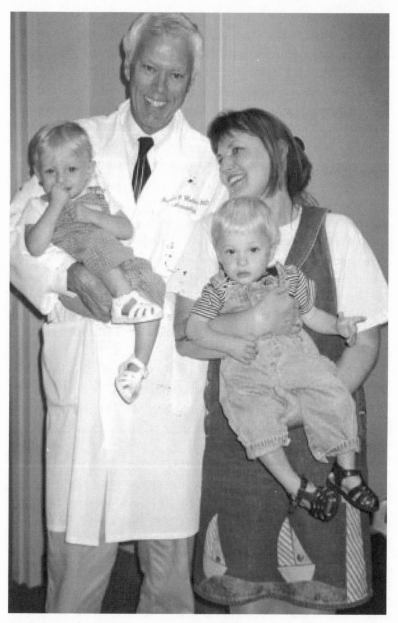

Dr. Hoekstra with Anna, Liam and nurse Lois Gilmore

now know some of their names—Lamarre and Simon and B. J. and Blake. Their experiences are here for us to contemplate. They do not settle everything—people will differ on what to make of their lives—but they should at the very least make us slow to declare what is possible and what is not.

Doctors must be more than conduits of expertise. A good doctor does much more than make medical decisions. He or she must enter into a partnership for healing that requires, on the relational level, a meeting between equals. Very little in the training of doctors or the organization of hospitals encourages this.

In the scientific model, truth is associated with objectivity. The more detached we are, the less, supposedly, we are subject to the errors of bias or emotion. This may work well for reading an x-ray, but it is disastrous for bringing healing to the whole person. Complete objectivity usually leads to treating people as objects.

One of the many times when a doctor must mix objectivity with simple humanity is when bringing bad news. No one is hungrier for news than the parents of a gravely ill child. One of the jobs of a doctor is to bear that news, and it is a heavy burden when the news is bad. Like all bearers of such information, doctors run the risk of directly or indirectly being blamed for the bad news they bring. More often the parents look to them for guidance and comfort.

Dr. Hoekstra feels keenly the responsibility of being both honest and compassionate. The latter includes the necessity of seeing each case afresh, the unique experience of a unique child born to parents who have likely never experienced anything remotely similar.

"I have dealt with thousands of parents over my two decades of working with newborns. I have to continually remind myself that none of these experiences is routine to the man and woman who have just become parents of an extremely premature infant. It's crucial that I empathize as best I can with their grief and anxiety."

The "as best I can" is a recognition that all grief is singular. The fingerprint of sorrow is never exactly replicated. Some suffer with stoic calm; others ask question after tearful question; a few drive around by themselves and scream at the freeways.

The ability to bring bad news in a healing way requires the willingness to be in the presence of suffering and to take some of it on yourself.

"You have to tell people in person. You shouldn't try to explain a serious situation over the phone. You need to meet with the family in a private setting where they feel it's safe to express their emotions. You have to sit down and take time with them. They are your first and only priority. They should be given all the time, attention and compassion they need."

A part of all good medical treatment is supportive human relationships, nowhere more so than with the greatly premature. Intense treatment extends over weeks and months; life and death crises occur and reoccur, linked by days of wearing routine. Data alone is not enough; parents need to feel they are working with people who value both them and their child, who are compassionate fellow human beings as well as expert technicians.

If people feel all this, then they can come to terms with any news, even the worst. But they must believe that they are being told the whole truth.

"Perhaps the first rule of giving bad news is to be totally honest. The situation must be explained in terms the family can understand. You have to repeatedly ask them if they are understanding the explanation being given and allow them to ask all the questions they need to ask."

If it is important to tell the family what you know, it is also important to tell them what you don't know. They need to understand the uncertainty inherent in all things dealing with the human condition—physical and otherwise. What seems true of an infant's condition today may not be true tomorrow. The likely outcome of any situation is not necessarily the actual outcome. These babies surprise us every day, both to our joy and to our sorrow.

Families also need to know that they can contact their physician easily and often, even after the child has been discharged from the hospital. They should not have the feeling that they are in the dark or on their own, especially when things are not going well. Dr. Hoekstra tries to maintain a delicate balance between optimism and realism, a balance that is rooted both in his faith and in his medical experience.

"It is crucial that the medical team not convey an attitude of giving up on a child because some major complication has developed. Parents need to be confident that everything possible will continue to be done for their child."

Even when everything possible is done, it sometimes is not enough. Anyone working in an NICU must at some time or other face the question of when treatment should be stopped.

Stopping treatment is not the same thing as giving up on life, or on the life of a specific child. In most cases it is, or should be, simply a recognition of our finitude. We do not create life, and beyond a certain point we cannot sustain life. We can encourage it, we can remove obstacles to it, but often we simply have to recognize what is happening and stand out of the way.

"I believe every infant should be given every chance possible to live, but clearly not every one will. Sometimes they are born with conditions that are simply not compatible with an extended life. We can prolong life for a while, but we cannot change what is inevitable."

Even if one acknowledges that *inevitable* is an imprecise word that sometimes masks our inability to imagine unforeseen outcomes, experience in the NICU teaches that certain conditions counsel the wise to prepare for disability or death. That does not mean, however, that there is no value in prolonging life even in catastrophic situations.

"Sometimes it's best for the sake of the parents to continue treatment for a time even when the child cannot be saved. It gives them a chance to understand the situation and to come to terms with it."

Consider, for instance, the tragic story of a woman's agonizing plea for someone to save the lives of her three babies. Dr. Hoekstra came on duty one day to find this woman in unstoppable labor with triplets. They knew she was exactly twenty-one and three-sevenths weeks pregnant, because they knew the exact date of her in vitro fertilization. The woman's husband had died two months after conception, and she was desperate to have his children, a physical manifestation of the life they had shared together.

One of the babies had already died in the womb. The mother was informed, as gently as possible, that there was genuinely no hope for the other two either. But when the second one came out with a heartbeat, the mother began to cry. She looked at Dr. Hoekstra and asked, "Won't you even try?"

What would you do? Would you consult the statistics? Ask the hospital ethics committee? Call the insurance company? Tell her how many other things you have to do that day?

Dr. Hoekstra tried to save them, knowing he couldn't. The third baby also was born alive. He spent the day working over them, all the time talking to the mother to help her see that they could not make it. They got progressively worse through the day, as was inevitable given the immaturity of their lungs.

"None of the other doctors openly criticized me, but I could see them looking at me cross-eyed. 'What are you doing?' But what else could I do?"

Nothing. There was nothing else he could have done and still be who he is. It cost thousands of dollars to keep those babies alive for those hours. It consumed his day. Was it all wasted?

"I have no regrets, because that mother will now have no regrets. She knows she did everything she could to save the lives of her dead husband's children. She'll never have to second-guess herself. She can be at peace about it."

What price should we put on a mother's peace?

＊　　＊　　＊

If then, to adapt Ecclesiastes, there is a time for extreme treatment, there is also a time when treatment should end.

Sometimes, despite our doing all that can be done, an infant's condition continues to deteriorate. When this goes on for a prolonged time and bodily failure begins to beget more failure, the question we raised in the Introduction must be asked. "Are we doing things *for* the baby, or are we simply doing things *to* the baby?"

Dr. Hoekstra is as committed to life as one could possibly be, but he recognizes that the same God who created life also created death—or at least the possibility. It is part of life as we find it. It is not only the inevitable end of each of us, it is the end God sometimes allows for the newest among us. When death is clearly at hand, and further treatment only means further suffering, then the possibility of stopping treatment must be considered. It can be as much an act of faith as the decision to treat to the very end.

"Rather than prolong the suffering of a baby who has no prospects for surviving, we will offer the parents the option of removing the infant from life support. But it is important that this option be an *offer* and not an order or directive. If parents don't want life support removed even in the face of continuing deterioration, then the infant is allowed to die on full life support."

Some people of faith condemn *any* cessation of treatment at *any* time. God can always do a miracle, the reasoning goes, and there is, therefore, no point at which one knows that death is inevitable. Treatment, therefore, can never rightly be discontinued.

It is, when you probe it, a somewhat puzzling position to take. It suggests that God isn't paying attention or can't make up his mind. It's as though God hasn't noticed up to now that this baby is seriously ill, so we need to keep things going for a few more hours or days so that he will awaken and act on the child's behalf.

Is it not a more mature faith to see that God has, of course, taken note, undoubtedly in sorrow, and that he has made a decision—if decision is the right word—a decision that is now being revealed to us. If God can perform a miracle at any time, as of course he can, there is nothing about stopping treatment that will prevent that miracle from happening.

"After everything has been tried and nothing helps, the humane thing is to allow the child to die in peace in the arms of the mother and father, rather than to die hooked up to rows of machines."

It is not only humane, it is also faithful.

Given the moral complexity and potential controversy surrounding any decision to stop treatment, it may be surprising to hear how easy the decision almost always is. Not *easy* in the sense of casual or painless or unprincipled, but easy in the sense of coming readily to a mutual understanding. This understanding is less about what to do, than about recognizing what is happening despite all that we have tried to do.

"If you establish a relationship with the family right at the beginning, then you can sit down with them when things appear to be futile and come to an agreement. I consider it one of the great blessings that, in almost all cases, God makes it clear when it's time to stop."

Dr. Hoekstra makes a crucial distinction, however, between discontinuing total support at the point of death and discontinuing it because of a severe complication that results from prematurity. If a baby must die because its body cannot support life, so be it. But if it must die because it is flawed, or because it will be difficult to care for, or, God forbid, because it is too expensive, then something is wrong.

"I don't believe that a severe complication means that we should withdraw support. A baby's physical and cognitive life does not have to be perfect to have value and meaning. I know that such an infant's life can place a family under great stress, but the child can also be a tremendous blessing and inspiration to a family and to others."

If perfection—or even complete mental, physical or spiritual health—is a requirement for life, which of us would not be in jeopardy? Many years ago I ran into a cocky young man who asserted that there was no rationally convincing argument for allowing the retarded to live. Since he was pursuing a graduate degree at the time, he obviously didn't feel personally at risk from such a policy. I pointed out to him that in a world organized by the kind of reasoning he espoused, there also would be a need for only a limited number of people with advanced degrees in his field. He might easily be judged expendable, perhaps even a burden to society. The fellow did not find my observation amusing. As I recall, he snorted and went away.

People like this fellow are growing in number and becoming bolder. They are usually practical people, reasonable people, people burdened with the best of intentions but unburdened with much sense of history or of moral depth. They are found more and more often in places of influence and power.

How much imperfection is too much imperfection? When is someone else's disability so profound that we feel qualified and within our rights to free that person from their disability through death? *Their* death, we must remember, not ours. The common argument, not without merit, is that the other person is suffering too much. Sometimes just beneath the surface of this argument, however, is the unstated premise, "*I* am suffering too much—and I will suffer more if I have to take care of this person."

At other times the argument takes the form, "I know I would not want to have to live under those circumstances; I am sure this person would not want to live like this either." This is a particularly chilling argument for those among us who are severely disabled but who nonetheless find their lives very much worth living. They can only be thankful that, up to this point, they have not had to make the case to anyone else for the value of their lives. The day may be coming when they will.

Stating the argument in this form and tone of course stacks the deck in favor of encouraging all life, no matter how damaged. And that, as is clear to anyone reading the stories in this book, is our bias. But encouraging life is just that, an encouragement, a coaxing, a searching for all possibilities for meaningful life. It is not a refusal to recognize when that search has come to an end. Parents, with their physicians, sometimes have agonizing choices to make regarding how much and how long to treat babies they have come to love with an intensity they did not know they possessed. The rest

of society has a right to be part of a general discussion of how we
should proceed in such cases, but we should never pretend that the
situation is anything but heartbreaking or that the right choices are
always crystal clear.

                          *   *   *

And then, of course, there is money. Here, as in so many areas of
modern life, money talks—more loudly all the time. We cannot
ignore the reality that someone has to pay. Who is willing to pay,
and how much, are growing factors in who lives and who dies.

Increasingly, the ones who pay directly are the HMOs (though of
course indirectly we are the ones who pay). Health maintenance
organizations are a fact of life in medical treatment these days and
an ever larger fact of life in the treatment of those born too soon. It
is the nature of HMOs—being businesses rather than charitable
organizations—to see a premature baby as an expense. This is not
unreasonable, but it can cause problems.

The problems do not usually begin at the initial moments of
great crisis, as Dr. Hoekstra observes.

"When a tiny, critically ill preemie arrives on the scene, there is
very little questioning that it belongs in a NICU. When that infant is
seen to be a survivor, however—when it has been weaned off a respirator, for instance—then a tug-of-war often begins."

HMOs frequently have contracts with what are called level two or
special care nurseries, which provide a less intense level of care
than the NICU. HMOs are anxious to have infants transferred to
such facilities because they are less expensive for the HMO. The
doctors, for a variety of reasons having to do with the infant's physical needs, may feel that such a transfer is not in the baby's best
interest.

Many times parents also feel uneasy about the proposed change,
for psychological as well as for medical reasons. The people in the
NICU are the ones who saved their baby. The parents have often

bonded to these people and even to the place. This is their baby's *home* until the hoped for day when the baby goes home for good.

The tug-of-war is sometimes subtle and sometimes not. HMOs have ways of making clear to the doctors within a practice that their future well being may be at stake.

"They will notify the doctor or the hospital that there are *other options* for placing such babies in the future if the doctors fail to perceive the need for *cooperation* on these issues."

It is a great irony that the richer we become as a nation, and at no time in human history has any nation been anywhere near so rich, the more we fret about whether we can *afford* to help those in greatest need.

The fact is, we can *afford* to do whatever it is we greatly *value* doing. If it is important to us as a society, we can and do choose to allocate our resources in such a way that money itself will not be the determining factor in accomplishing what we desire. To adapt Shakespeare, "The fault lies not with our treasuries, but with ourselves."

A common argument is that the money spent to save the lives of the severely premature would save even more lives if it were spent on things like general prenatal care, immunizations or even alleviating malnutrition. This is factually true but ignores another fact in the real world: money saved in one area does not necessarily, or even usually, flow to another area where it is more needed.

Our country experienced this cold reality, for instance, at the end of the Vietnam War. Countless articles were written about the so-called "peace dividend." Many of them offered long lists of all the good that could and would be accomplished by the money saved from the military budget when the war was over. The war did end, but the military budget did not go down, and few if any of those good things that should have been possible came about.

One sees similar lists today regarding all that could be done with the money saved if we simply quit trying to save these problematic children. Are we really to believe that if the HMOs did not have to pay for Lamarre or Blake there would suddenly be more money in the national budget for immunizations or vitamins for mothers? Those programs deserve more money, but it is going to come because we as a society decide it is important to fund them, not because we turn off respirators in the NICU.

It is a mistake to allow good and necessary things to be pitted against each other in a false either-or choice—preemies or immunizations, respirators or prenatal screening. Why not set *both* against what we spend in our society on video games, aircraft carriers, running shoes and cat food?

The cost of medical treatment is a serious problem. The search for ways of controlling cost is laudable and necessary. But we cross a critical line in our civilization when the question of the value of a life is not answered before a glance at the budget. It is a line we crossed decades ago when we accepted the argument that a particular child at a particular time is unaffordable and therefore rightly terminated. The line had been crossed even before this, and it has been crossed many times since.

For a growing number, the line no longer exists. Everything—absolutely everything—has a price tag. This is not good news for people at either end of life, or for many in between. Someone, somewhere, has an idea of how much money you're worth. It's a matter of charts and graphs, an objective calculation—no offense intended. And someday, when the balance between our worth and the cost of maintaining us tilts the wrong way, we may find the numbers disappointing.

*   *   *

The stories of the babies told in this book have been stories greatly shaped by faith. Dr. Hoekstra's own faith is central to what defines him. He is not conspicuously pious. He does not seek to evangelize strangers in parks or at bus stops. But he cannot think of who he is or why he is here without thinking of God.

"I start with the belief that God is real and that he is interested and involved in what I do. I am not what you would call a saint, not even sanctified. But I do believe that God has seen fit to work through me, as he does through many people. I believe that directly or indirectly God has given me the knowledge and wisdom to do my job the way he wants me to do it. I believe God honors your efforts when you give him the credit."

Dr. Hoekstra knows this outlook makes him more than a little strange to some people, including to some with whom he works. He doesn't try to convince them he is right. Rather he does his job the best he can by the light of his own convictions.

One of those convictions is that God does, in fact, intervene in the affairs of men and women—and of babies.

"When you talk about faith and medicine at the same time, people always want to know if you believe in miracles. When I consider a dictionary definition of *miracle* as an extraordinary event manifesting divine intervention in human affairs, I have no doubt whatsoever that I have seen many miracles in my twenty years of working in neonatology. I have seen God do so many incredible things that I am honestly not so surprised by it anymore."

Dr. Hoekstra's view is consistent with that of Mother Madeleine Mary.

"A miracle is not magic. You don't pray to manipulate God. Most people think of miracles as something against nature, but I think maybe that's because we don't really understand nature as God has made it. I believe a miracle happens because it will reveal God's presence for someone when they need it. It happens when it needs to happen for the kingdom of God to unfold—the kingdom that is within you."

Dr. Hoekstra has no doubt that he has witnessed miraculous interventions in the lives of his patients, but, like Mother Madeleine Mary, he is not sure what brings them about or why they seem to happen in some cases and not in others.

"Many families pray for specific healing and miracles. Certainly the Scriptures encourage that. Others pray in general terms that God's will is done, hoping of course that God's will coincides with their own hopes."

Dr. Hoekstra tends more toward the latter kind of prayer himself, but he wonders if it demonstrates weakness.

"I often wonder if I am lacking faith when I pray for God's will to be done, which makes any outcome seem an answer to prayer rather than praying for a specific healing and even miracle for my patients and their families. Do miracles not happen because I doubt they will happen? I pray more for specifics now."

He also is concerned, or used to be, about how the families who pray for healing would take it when physical healing did not take place.

"I used to worry about what would happen to the faith of these people if they didn't get their miracle, so to speak. Would their faith collapse or perhaps just wither away?"

This is not an idle concern. Many people have a cost-benefit kind of faith. I do this for God (go to church, tithe, pray, be a good person) and God does this for me (health, happiness, security, prosperity). A significant break in the perceived benefits can result in marked decline in the acts and attitudes of faith.

In fact, however, Dr. Hoekstra has found the opposite more often the case.

"I learned my worries were foolish. The lives of these people 'came forth as gold.' In the time of their great need, so many of them experienced a gift of strength from God to continue on. Their faith and trust in God's grace was stronger than ever."

Many families testify to the great blessing Dr. Hoekstra has been in their lives. B. J.'s mom is not the only one to suspect he came into their lives at God's direction. Again, Dr. Hoekstra sees the blessing as the other way around.

"Over the years I have had the wonderful privilege to be involved in the lives of countless people in their hour of greatest crisis. I can truthfully say that most have ministered to me more than I have ministered to them."

This sense of blessing flowing both ways has not depended on everything turning out well for the infant physically.

"I have observed incredible faith in families who asked God for a miracle and then watched that miracle occur. I have also seen families with equally amazing faith who prayed for a specific miracle that did not occur. I believe God is sovereign and that he exercises his will in both cases. God uses both good and bad outcomes—as judged by our human perspective—to draw people to himself."

God also uses human beings. Dr. Hoekstra does not claim to understand fully the relationship between faith and healing, or between faith and death, though he has seen a lot of both. He also understands that his very belief that there is a relation between these things and faith makes him strange in the medical world. No more strange, however, than the miraculous lives of these little ones born too soon.

CHAPTER SEVEN

LESSONS IN LIVING

"Man tells you the facts, but God tells you the truth."

TRACEY HAGMAN

"There are three things that will endure—faith, hope, and love—and the greatest of these is love."

1 CORINTHIANS 13:13 NLT

W hen we want to preserve something too important to be lost, we put it in a story. Here we have five stories of five families and six children. What do we learn from these five stories? What more do we know now that we know of Lamarre, and Simon, and B. J., and Blake, and Anna and Liam? Each person will take away something different. Some will find their basic values confirmed, others challenged. Our hope is that everyone will see more clearly the potential for great significance even in the shortest lives.

When we look at these young lives, we see in microcosm the human qualities that make for greatness and the human limitations that make for brokenness and broken hearts. We see ordinary people in extraordinary circumstances that both test who they are and give them the opportunity to become much more than they ever thought they could be.

No child is ever sick alone. When a newborn is at risk over a long period, so are the parents, and the family, and a widening complex of relationships. Also at risk are whole value systems and ways of understanding the world. Sometimes the risk results in growth and deepening and new strength. Other times it leads to disintegration and conflict and collapse. Often it results in some of both.

Long-term crises will weigh you and show where you are wanting. They will reveal where you are strong and where you are weak, both as an individual and in your relationships. You will be surprised by your strength. You will be surprised by your weakness. You will also be surprised by the number of people willing to help.

*   *   *

One thing to be learned from those born too soon is perseverance. Perseverance is continuing in a direction despite unfavorable circumstances. It is taking another step when the last ten each seemed impossible.

Perseverance is trying for the seventh or eighth time to put Liam's feeding tube down his throat, finally succeeding, then having him throw it up—and starting over. It is jumping into the car for the hundredth time to race through traffic to have fifteen minutes with B. J. for lunch. It is taking Lamarre's long list of problems and, over the months, checking them off one by one.

Perseverance is an admirable quality precisely because it has so little immediate reward. By definition, perseverance is not the singular heroic act that wins applause, nor the moment of crisis that calls for everyone's best. It is the dulling, energy-consuming, emotion-sapping need to do yet again what one has done over and over before.

Perseverance is suctioning out the mucus, not only in the middle of the night, but for the fourth or fifth time in a night. You do it because if you don't, your baby will not be able to breathe. You do it because it is there to be done, and there is no one else to do it.

In one sense there is nothing automatically praiseworthy about perseverance with newborns. What other choice do you have? It's not really like the choice between getting up early to jog or staying in bed for an extra thirty minutes. If you don't jog, you get a little paunchier. If you don't suction mucus, your baby dies. So you do what you have to do.

What is praiseworthy in the perseverance of these parents is the nobility with which they endure. *Nobility* is not too high a word. It doesn't mean they do not sometimes crack, sometimes despair, sometimes even whine a bit. It means that despite the occasional lapse, they continue to reach deep inside themselves for a strength they didn't know they had. And that strength, displayed over time, gives them a kind of calm dignity that is rightly called nobility.

The strength of character that we call perseverance is gained in the same way as muscular strength—through a pattern of repeated exertions over time. Lift weights many times over a long period and you will end up with strong and shapely muscles. Repeatedly exercise your will in the direction of serving another and you will build a strength of spirit that can stand the strong winds of life.

*   *   *

These stories also teach us something about suffering. Suffering results from the gap between how things should be and how they are. Because we are able to conceive of wholeness, we suffer from its lack. Because we can imagine a heaven, or a heaven on earth, we suffer for the world's fallenness. Because we know what a healthy baby is, we grieve for one who needs a ventilator to breathe.

Ultimately, we suffer because we love. These children born before their time teach us to love, and because we love them we suffer, and because we suffer we love even more. If we do not care about something or someone, nothing that happens to them will hurt us. On the other hand, the more we value them, the more they can cause us pain.

The deepest kind of love, then, is suffering love. You cannot love someone without placing yourself at risk, and with risk comes the likelihood of pain. B. J. was not the only one at risk during the early months of his life. So also were Alliette and Bennie and their girls, for they took the chance of loving a son and brother who might be taken away.

This link between love and suffering strikes at something fundamental about the nature of God and of the human experience. At the center of the Christian faith is a cross, an emblem of suffering and of love, and of the mysterious joining of the two together. It was literally and symbolically the place Alliette went to when she couldn't carry the pain of B. J.'s decline any further. Suffering love was what each of these parents felt when they held the tiny hands of their children in the isolettes.

Suffering either destroys or deepens us. It cannot leave us the same. Each of these parents would have spared their children and themselves the pain if they could have. Each of them is a more profound person because they could not.

Suffering deepens us because it strips away superficiality. It is an acid that dissolves pettiness, complacency, smugness and triviality. It is the single greatest force for reordering priorities in the world. Suffering is a great clarifier. It clarifies what is real and what is artificial, what is precious and what is worthless, what is lasting and what is passing away.

How can Tracey worry about the latest dress style when Simon is having another cardiac arrest? How can Anthony angle for a nicer office at work when Lamarre has bleeding in the brain? How can Leslie listen to petty gossip when Blake may be going blind? How can any of them value anything this world has to offer more highly than the love and prayers and practical help of family and friends?

✻   ✻   ✻

The suffering we have seen in these stories teaches us that pain is not meant to be endured alone. Through their experiences, each of these couples has learned something about community. It has been argued that when we are in great pain, we do not need theological explanations *of* it but help getting *through* it. That help can come from many places, but it comes best from a community of people prepared to be the hands and voice of God to one of God's children.

In the case of Simon's parents, the links to the community of faith were already strong, and the community was engaged before the crises peaked. With Tina and Laurie, there was not only no community initially, there was not even much understanding of what a community was or how it could work. They had to discover both a community they did not know existed in a nearby church and to rediscover the resources available from Tina's grandmother's community that had always been available to them.

Each of these people also found there is a community available within the NICU—doctors who care, nurses who are caring, chaplains and social workers to be advocates with God and Caesar, and other parents who are walking the same path. Jewel found Tracey after Anthony noticed all the Christian trappings around Simon's isolette. Tracey and Alliette had linked up earlier. Each of them held up the other. Each of them *suffered with* the other and therefore each of them suffered less, or less despairingly, than they would have otherwise.

Perhaps the greatest blessing in community these couples discovered was the community of two represented by their marriage. They were blessed, as is often not the case with premature babies, with marriages that stood the test. They illustrate the truth of the passage in Ecclesiastes about the advantage of standing together, especially with God as a third:

> Two people are better off than one, for they can help each other succeed. If one person falls, the other can reach out and help. But someone who falls alone is in real trouble. Likewise, two people lying close together can keep each other warm. But how can one be warm alone? A person standing alone can be attacked and defeated, but

two can stand back-to-back and conquer. Three are even better, for a triple-braided cord is not easily broken. (Eccles 4:9-12 NLT)

We shouldn't talk about the community of a marriage, however, without including the other children in a family touched by the birth of a premature child. Bennal and Burgette didn't feel the need for a brother, but when B. J. came, they hoped he would never leave. Leave he did, but not before teaching them things they need to know, like Burgette's observation, "B. J. made me realize that life is precious and taught me not to take things for granted."

And then there's Sammy, the brother who didn't want to share his BaBa with Simon. What does Sammy think now that his brother is home?

"It's pretty good, because I love him a lot. And he does this to me. I'll show you."

With this, Sammy takes Simon in his lap on the floor. They sit face to face, their legs intertwined, and reach forward and embrace, each smiling and patting the other on the back.

"He does this to me, and I really like it."

Of course, it's one thing to love your brother in the privacy of your own home. But might not a brother with a line running out of his throat to a machine be a little embarrassing when you're in the park? After all, kids can be cruel when someone is perceived as different. Tracey is happy to report that this is not the case with Sammy.

"Whenever we go to the park or anywhere, he is the first to say, 'Come and meet my brother, Simon. This is Simon—this is my brother.'"

"This is Simon—this is my brother." How does one calculate the value of that when determining who should be saved and at what cost?

These couples also discovered that community includes strangers. At every turn, they came across strangers who cared—a dispatcher who made it his business to get Anna and Liam home, a couple in China who prayed for Simon, a mother of a blind child willing to be a resource for Blake. There is a saying that strangers are simply friends we have not yet met. Perhaps there's more truth to it than a cynical world normally concedes.

*   *   *

Pain and suffering are unavoidably a part of life with the greatly premature, making perseverance a necessity. But so are hope and joy. Hope is more than wishing. It is the determination to focus on the real possibilities for a good outcome without denying the real possibilities for a bad one. It can be based on faith in medicine, in God, or both. It may grow out of one's basic temperament or past experiences in life. Or it may come from seeing other kids make it who are just as threatened. Blake's pediatrician said, "Blake is my hope story." Everyone needs such a story and for hope to be part of his or her own story.

The hope that arises from faith in God is different from other kinds of hope. It is based on an understanding of all of reality, not only of the particular circumstances of this moment in time. It sees the universe as infused with benevolence. It believes there are purpose and meaning to what, from another point of view, seems randomness and chaos.

This kind of hope does not require temporal success. It can remain hopeful despite the loss of all that is hoped for. It can coexist with death.

Such hope is possible because it sees all things, death included, from the perspective not of time but of eternity. If there is a loving and just God who welcomes back to himself all his creatures, then one's hope does not depend on this or that outcome. It depends on the character of God, the one who can turn all outcomes to good.

Joy also comes in different sizes. It can be Tracey's first peek at Simon's tape-covered nose, or the much deeper joy that comes from her realization that Simon is ultimately in the hands of the one who both made and loves him.

Joy is the stab—or gentle stream—of emotional and spiritual pleasure that comes from being right with the world. It can burst out in a brief eruption at hearing Simon's first sound without a ventilator or at the word that B. J. has grown enough bowel to live. But at its deepest, joy is a quiet delight at being at peace with all that is.

For this reason, joy is not to be confused with happiness. Happiness is a transient emotional state that can coincide with joy but is not its equal. No one could feel happy the morning B. J. lost his battle for life. But one could feel joy in what B. J. had meant to those who came to love him. One could feel joy that he was returning to his maker, having accomplished those things he was created to do.

Joy can be a companion of sadness. Sadness is not weakness or lack of faith. It flows from our longing for wholeness, a longing put in our hearts by God. We are right to be sad at the pain and brokenness and death in the world. God shares that sadness. It should not, however, overpower our confident hope that wholeness wins out in the end, nor defeat the joy that such a hope brings.

*   *   *

One could discuss many other lessons for living that grow out of these stories. There are lessons in courage, mercy, humility and prayer. But all these and more are in the stories themselves and do not require further abstract discussion.

Honesty requires, however, recognizing that other emotions are also part of these stories—anger, frustration, bewilderment, depression, discouragement and despair. If these things were not present, these stories would not be real. They certainly wouldn't be stories about human beings.

Sometimes the anger is directed at doctors or friends or loved ones. Sometimes it is directed at God. Sometimes it is just a generalized shaking of the fist at the sky—at the "way things are," at a world in which the innocent can suffer. Sometimes it is directed inward at ourselves.

Despair is the opposite of perseverance. It says, "No, I can't go any further. I won't go any further. This is more than I can bear. It is more than anyone should have to bear, and I won't. I will no longer work and hope with so little reward."

The discouraging thing about despair is that the natural universe does not care about your despair. Your declaration that you can't take it any more does not result in any change in your circumstances. In Samuel Beckett's famous absurdist play *Waiting for Godot* one character announces, "I can't go on like this." His companion bleakly responds, "That's what you think."

Fortunately, God understands despair. It was Christ, you remember, who in the extremity of his suffering—physical and spiritual—asked the bleakest question of all, "My God, my God! Why have you forsaken me?" If Christ could ask that question, you and I can ask ours.

Any faith purporting to be adequate to the human experience must be one that can accommodate anger, frustration, bewilderment, depression, discouragement and despair. In their own way, each person represented in these stories found such a faith. For some it was a continuation of a faith they already had, for others it was a deepening in an existing faith that had not been tested, for still others it was a first experience with faith whose final contours are yet undecided.

No one is the same after experiences such as these, and neither are their understandings of God. All of them, for instance, pray differently now than they did before. They pray more specifically, more confidently, more boldly approaching God with their hearts' desires.

Tracey's experience with Simon, for instance, has enlarged her expectations of God and of herself.

"God wants you to believe him for God-sized things. And he wants you to ask. God loves us and did not give us a spirit of timidity, but of power and love and self-discipline. He wants us to approach his throne with boldness, because we are children of the king. I've gone from focusing on healing so much to focusing on how much God loves us, and how much he wants to perform miracles in our lives if we will only ask."

Tracey also has a whole new appetite for reading the Bible. In her journal she sometimes wrote out verses with Simon's name inserted, or put herself into a verse that promised God's support and victory. But while she puts herself in the Bible, she also talks of putting the Bible inside herself.

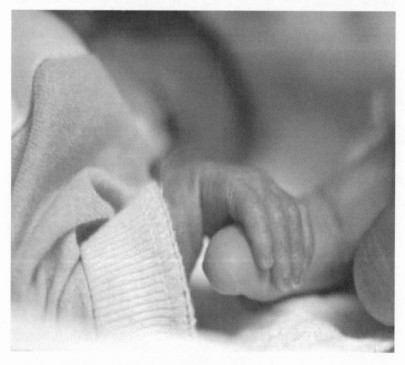

Anna at two weeks holds Laurie's finger in the NICU

"I fell in love with the Bible. I felt like I literally wanted to eat it. I'd cover my face and head with it during my quiet times. God showed me it was alive and active. It jumped off of the page at me. I started memorizing the Bible to have it in my mind while I was with Simon at the hospital. On one of the days he almost died, the verse came to me that says, 'Our God is a God who saves; from the sovereign Lord comes escape from death.' I learned that man tells you the facts, but God tells you the truth."

Faith, hope and love—these are at the center of reality. Without them life has no meaning. But even with them life is hard—as the stories of Lamarre, and Simon, and B. J., and Blake, and Anna and Liam testify. No search for meaning and beauty in their stories should erase the stubborn fact that their lives, and the lives of those to whom they were entrusted, have been hard. Any significant accomplishment involves pain, and these lives were, above all else, significant.

*   *   *

We began this book with Lamarre, and we will end with Lamarre. Jewel and Anthony joyfully took him home when he was ten months old. He still had a shunt in his head to relieve pressure in his brain, but he was home and there was hope. Over the next year he was in and out of the hospital for various problems, from stomach ailments to infections. Therapists came regularly to his home, and he was making progress.

When he was twenty-two months old, however, things began to go bad. Lamarre had a major hemorrhage in his brain, the first since the beginning of his life. The position of his shunt was changed two or three times. He began to have seizures and tremors. The doctor said his brain stem was starting to be affected.

Around this time Jewel's father died unexpectedly. While she was gone to Ohio for his funeral, Lamarre got worse and was admitted back into the hospital on Father's Day. For the first time he was in the PICU, the pediatric intensive care unit, as Jewel recalls.

"We knew then it was very serious, because only the sickest little kids go into PICU. He was put on a respirator for the first time since he was tiny. He was on life support, not doing anything on his own."

Lamarre's liver had been damaged from being fed intravenously all his life. As a result the liver was swollen in size and pushing up on his lungs, making breathing difficult. He also had a plum-sized blood clot pressing against his kidneys, making it hard for him to urinate.

These multiple organ failures made Lamarre sicker than he had ever been, and his prospects for survival shrank. Anthony struggled with watching his son deteriorate.

"I was to the point of not knowing how much longer I could see him in this condition. It got hard. I had never seen him like that. He didn't open his eyes. When we touched him to comfort him, he would react, and the buzzers would go off, but he didn't open his eyes."

Jewel wasn't ready to concede anything.

"I still hadn't experienced in the natural sense what God would or would not do for Lamarre if we continued to confess and believe in him. I didn't want to sway. I believed if I continued to press on, that God would reveal to us what would happen. I was always in a position of not being the one to surrender. I would persevere with Lamarre until the end, whatever end that would be. I wasn't going to tell the Lord how this was going to unfold. I just wanted to walk through it."

The doctor was sure the walk wouldn't be much longer. He explained to them about code three resuscitation, in which an all-out effort is made to bring back a patient who has stopped breathing. He asks Anthony and Jewel repeatedly if they want such efforts for Lamarre. They tell him the same thing they said two years earlier when Lamarre was first born and there was so much skepticism about his survival. "As long as Lamarre will receive it, then you go ahead and give it."

One summer day in August, when Lamarre had been in intensive care for more than six weeks, Anthony and Jewel spent the whole day with him, as Anthony remembers.

"It was just a beautiful day. We had this Christian music playing from the radio, and it was so peaceful. Just a great day. One of Jewel's friends came in about eleven that night to pray with us and to encourage us. After she left, sometime after midnight, I told Jewel I was going to lie down for a while, and I went and found a sleep room in the hospital."

Jewel stayed with Lamarre.

"I was sitting there sometime after two in the morning quoting healing verses to Lamarre when the buzzers and alarms started going off. The nurses came running into the room. It was a code three alert, the first one Lamarre had ever had. One of the nurses turned to me and said, 'Go get your husband. Go get your husband!'"

Jewel had difficulty finding which sleep room Anthony was in. When they got back, the nurses were performing CPR on Lamarre. The doctor arrived a few minutes later.

"Everyone was working around Lamarre, and the doctor was watching the monitors. After a while he just said, 'Stop' and everybody stopped. I said to him, 'Why did you do that?' and he said, 'There's nothing else we can do.' He never said Lamarre had died, only 'There's nothing else we can do.'"

Nothing else we can do—an appropriate admission of human limitations. Lamarre *had* died, and there was nothing else this doctor could do. But there was one more thing Jewel and Anthony could do, and, characteristically, it involved a slight bending of standard hospital procedures.

"The doctor turned to Anthony and me and said, 'If you and your husband will step out, the nurses will prepare him, and then you can come back in.' And I said, 'No, you all can leave, and we will take care of our son.'"

And so they did. They took the tube out of his mouth, then washed him up. They put oil on him and clean clothes.

"We had washed him every night of his life, and this was the same. Dr. Hoekstra used to say we had him shining like a brand new penny, and that's what we did one more time."

Anthony held and rocked Lamarre while Jewel changed the bed and collected his things. A nurse came in and took a picture of them holding him, then left.

"Then Anthony gave Lamarre to me, and I rocked him. No one else was in the room. Then Anthony and I both laid him to rest in the bed together. We tucked a blanket around him. He was just lying there shining."

When everything was finally done, they pushed backed the curtains that had been pulled around his bed in the unit. It was after three in the morning, and the rest of the room was dark. No one was there—no doctors, no nurses, no chaplain, no social worker—nobody. Anthony felt abandoned.

"There was no one there to say a thing to us. You talk about an empty feeling. It was the emptiest feeling of my life. No one was there. You are on your own."

To make matters worse, they had driven separate cars to the hospital that day. So in the darkest time of the night, in the darkest night of their lives, after the death of their only child, they each drove home alone—in a heavy rain. Jewel cried hard for the first time.

"I just started crying and crying. It was a wailing cry. It was a hard rain, with the windshield wipers going fast, and I was wailing. I couldn't hardly see."

One thing she could see was this was not the way it should end.

"When we walked out of that hospital and didn't see anybody, I knew then it was not over. I still had work to do for the Lord. I knew it was going to go on, but I didn't know it would be within eight hours."

Amazingly, or maybe not, Jewel and Anthony decided to go to church that morning. What better place to be? After a few hours' sleep they went to their church. They told the pastor that Lamarre had died a few hours before, and the pastor embraced them and prayed with them. The sermon that Sunday was on looking toward the future, not the past.

After the service they met with some of the people who had
interceded for them in prayer over the two years of Lamarre's life.
They prayed for an hour in the church and then one of the women
asked them a question. "Do you want to go back to Children's Hospital?"

Why did the woman suggest going back to the hospital only
hours after they had left their dead son there? Anthony answers
with a smile.

"We had undone business."

They had left in the night feeling empty and alone. They were
coming back at noon with what Anthony called "a caravan of intercessory warriors." Jewel felt the same.

"I felt like we were soldiers in the army for the Lord. We were
marching in, all dressed up in our church clothes."

They presented themselves to the receptionist in the lobby. It
was a day the receptionist will not soon forget.

"I said, 'We're here to see Lamarre Foster. He's in the morgue.'
Her eyes got so huge. The receptionist pushed back on the wheels
of her chair and ran to get a supervising nurse."

The supervising nurse came out and indicated they had never
had a request like this before, but if everyone would like to wait in a
room, she would see what could be done. About twenty minutes
later she returned and said Lamarre would be brought to a post-
operation recovery room.

They went into the room where a circle of rocking chairs had
been placed. The nurse brought in Lamarre, wrapped in blankets.
Jewel indicated that he should be given to his father. Anthony
remembers what was essentially a spiritual party in honor of Lamarre's life.

"You talk about celebrating life. It was a total celebration of
Lamarre's life—a total contrast to the night before. God had
unfolded for us to come with our intercessory prayer warriors, and
the brothers and sisters, and just make a joyful noise unto the Lord.
They heard us wailing and praising in there, and they wondered

what in the world was going on."

Whatever was going on, it went on for nearly three hours. They didn't use the rocking chairs much, preferring like David to walk and dance before the Lord. They tired out their bodies but not their spirits, as Jewel remembers.

"We finally sat down to rest. We were laughing and talking and sharing about how God had blessed us. They said we were prime examples of people who were not living in the natural realm. 'Otherwise you couldn't be sitting there holding your son and praising God.'"

From the very beginning some people felt Jewel and Anthony were simply running from reality in how they conceived of Lamarre and his possibilities. The Fosters always thought it was the opposite. They were running *to* reality. And Anthony didn't see it any differently now that Lamarre had died.

"It had been a supernatural, spectacular event from his birth, and it ended the same way it had begun. So it was hard to look at it as a loss. It was not a natural event. It was something special that we were a part of. Lamarre is with us. We are spirits. We still feel Lamarre's spirit. Absent from the body is present with the Father. Life is a dream, and heaven is the reality—and that's where we are all trying to get. We live in the spiritual realm."

Jewel adds, "The Lord had allowed us to be part of this unveiling. We celebrated Lamarre's life from the beginning to the end, and we had miracles in between."

And this was the message they wanted to convey at Lamarre's memorial service. He was interred back in Ohio, surrounded by the graves of departed grandparents and other family. A memorial service was held in Minneapolis. Anthony wanted it clearly understood that Lamarre was much more than the sum of his medical problems.

"We wanted to show it wasn't a tragedy. It wasn't just wear and tear and grind over all those months. It was a supernatural experience, and we wanted everyone to experience that too. He wasn't just what they call a 'fragile infant' with multiple medical conditions. He was so much more than that. We wanted to share how much we loved our child, how much joy he gave us, how much joy he gave to the medical staff. The memorial service was mainly for the hospital staff and for our friends—our extended family, the people who had supported us."

Many from the hospital—staff and parents of other children—were at the service. The program had pictures of Lamarre at various stages of his journey, one with a winning smile on his face. The service opened with a song, "The Lord is Gonna Give You Rest," followed by the reading of a passage from the book of Romans (8:31-39 KJV).

> If God *be* for us, who *can be* against us? He that spared not his own Son, but delivered him up for us all, how shall he not with him also freely give us all things? . . .
>
> Who shall separate us from the love of Christ? *shall* tribulation, or distress, or persecution, or famine, or nakedness, or peril, or sword? . . .
>
> Nay, in all these things we are more than conquerors through him that loved us. For I am persuaded, that neither death, nor life, nor angels, nor principalities, nor powers, nor things present, nor things to come, Nor height, nor depth, nor any other creature, shall be able to separate us from the love of God, which is in Christ Jesus our Lord.

A series of men and women from the pastoral staff spoke in turn. One cited the example of David who wept and fasted and prostrated himself for seven days for the life of his sick child, refusing to heed the advice of those around him. When the child died, David's servants were afraid to tell him for fear he would harm himself. But he surprised them by taking the news calmly. He got up, washed himself, changed his clothes, and went to the house of the Lord to worship. Then he returned home and ate, saying to his questioning servants, "While the child was yet alive, I fasted and wept: for I said, Who can tell *whether* God will be gracious to me, that the child may live? But now he is dead, wherefore should I fast? can I bring him back again? I shall go to him, but he shall not return to me" (2 Sam 12:22-23 KJV).

This is an apt story for Jewel and Anthony in many ways. They fought for Lamarre's life with all their strength and faith. They spoke with confidence, even defiance, that he would be healed. Those who did not share their faith thought they were deluded. Even those who did share their faith worried that they and their faith would be shattered if Lamarre did not make it.

Both were wrong. Jewel and Anthony accepted Lamarre's death with the same grace that they had accepted the challenge of his life. Like David, they returned home and washed themselves and changed their clothes, and then they went to the house of the Lord to worship.

Another pastor pointed out that Lamarre's life encourages us to understand correctly who we are as human beings. He paraphrased the Catholic theologian Teilhard de Chardin. "We mistakenly think we are human beings trying to have a spiritual experience. In reality we are spiritual beings who have a brief human experience. Lamarre mastered his human experience in two years. The rest of us are still working on it."

Tracey, Simon's mother, also spoke, a representative of the many whose lives had been touched by Lamarre's life.

"God is in the business of miracles, and Lamarre had many in his life. We are going to miss Lamarre so much. It was a privilege to know him. He encouraged my faith. Lamarre taught me there are some things only God can do."

Jewel and Anthony chose to speak as well. They thanked people for sharing Lamarre's life with them, they expressed their gratitude for the privilege of being his parents, and they expressed their love for each other. Anthony chose a boxing analogy.

"Muhammad Ali once said that of all the people he had fought in his career, Sonny Liston was the scariest. And he said George Foreman was the strongest. But he said, 'If I had to storm the gates of hell, the person I would want by my side would be Joe Frazier.' "

Joe Frazier was a tenacious fighter who always moved forward, no matter how much he was battered. He was undiscourageable. Anthony needed someone like this beside him.

"And God gave me just such a mate and friend in Jewel. I couldn't have had someone any less than her and made it through this."

Jewel also expressed her gratitude for God giving her a strong man like Anthony to protect and support her, and she made it clear that she was not in the mood for sympathy cards.

"I don't want anyone to pity us. Be happy for us. Be happy for the strength of the Lord and the way he has sustained us. This is not a tragedy. It was an honor and privilege to take care of Lamarre. It was an honor that God chose Anthony and me to be his parents. Lamarre was a true joy."

Anthony and Jewel have a new reason for joy. As the date for Lamarre's second birthday approached, the first since his death, they were concerned about how they were going to feel and how to spend the day. Should they go out of town? Should they try to be with friends? Alone?

A few days before the birthday, Jewel noticed she had no appetite. She took a long lunch break and went to the doctor. It was Father's Day weekend, exactly a year since Lamarre had gone into the hospital for the last time, and Jewel discovered that Anthony was going to be a father again. They had wondered how they were going to spend Lamarre's birthday. They spent it celebrating a new life.

Typically, Jewel sees it in biblical terms.

"We are told, God will give you a double portion for your trouble. We will welcome the new one with open arms."

And Anthony adds, "And we will tell the new child about big brother Lamarre."

* * *

Five stories of five families and of six children—Lamarre, Simon, B. J., Blake, and Anna and Liam—some with happy endings, some with sad, but all worthy of the telling. And of the living. When reduced to its simplest, the central fact of each of their lives is that they mattered. They were and are valuable in ways beyond prediction and beyond counting and beyond comprehension. The world is better for each of them having been with us.